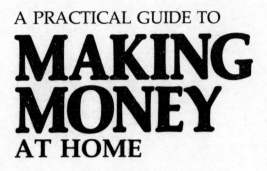

A PRACTICAL GUIDE TO

# MAKING
# MONEY
## AT HOME

# A PRACTICAL GUIDE TO
# MAKING MONEY
## AT HOME

OLGA FRANKLIN

BOOK CLUB ASSOCIATES
LONDON

First published in Great Britain in 1977
This edition published 1982 by
Book Club Associates
by arrangement with
Macdonald & Co
London & Sydney

Photoset by
Rowland Phototypesetting Ltd.
Bury St Edmunds, Suffolk.
Printed in Great Britain by
Hazell, Watson & Viney Ltd
Aylesbury, Bucks.

# Contents

# Introduction

This book is designed to enable you to make a decent living at home, at a time when it has become more difficult to make one outside it.

The decline in big business now means that many of us get a Second Chance in life, to choose work we like better – which is the reason for my book, with its variety of opportunities to inspire you to become your own Boss. Some people are hesitant, fearing they lack the self-discipline needed to go it alone. Yet often they are the very people who turn into successful home-based tycoons once they've found the work that suits them.

When I wrote the first edition of this book four years ago the economic situation was different. Today people are realistic. They're ready to recognise that the freelance way of life may be the best road to recovery. They know that even when the 'Recession' ends there won't be enough jobs to go round – because of that threatened 'micro-chip revolution' when we might all be out of work.

Of course if you live on Mr Roy Plomley's desert island or in the Outer Hebrides it would be much harder to make a living, because of an acute shortage of customers; or because transport costs to your far-away customers would be uneconomic. Luckily most of our customers are almost next door and will love us for keeping strictly to the delivery dates promised.

One of the good things about the present-day squeeze on business is the redundancy money. No one had *that* last depression-time round. Keep firm hold of it, to spend later on the tools, equipment, even premises (if the money will stretch that far) for your new Home Business.

Another good thing about the recession (now don't shout please – at least, not until you've read to the end of my intro . . .) it reveals in starkest detail just *what* goods, what services people really want. I mean, who needs a High Street with four greengrocers and five footwear emporiums? So your task of deciding what kind of business you'll choose is made much simpler. What have they *not* got in your street or block of flats?

I also realise there are people who dread 'getting stuck inside the house all day'. It's said to be one of Society's fast-growing social problems, like alcoholism and smoking. But my ideas for making-money-at-home do *not* mean you are tied to the house 24 hours a day. On the contrary, it is good for you to try to go right outside your home for one, two, three or even four hours a day if possible and if the work you choose calls for it. The whole idea of home-based work is to broaden your life, so I have included all kinds of jobs, where you can either go out to do them for a couple of hours a day, and meet people, or you can have a shorter but more efficient working day inside the home, leaving you free to go out afterwards.

I realise that for some people the whole point of going out to work was to meet people. They like the company! So please don't be put off by any fears of isolation. Of course you'll miss the company . . . the tea breaks . . . not to mention the Luncheon Vouchers! But once you get going I think you'll make plenty of friends when you go out, perhaps for a couple of hours a day or more, to call on customers, buy your new equipment, show your samples, flog your knitting . . . or even just go out to bring the money in. . . . There never was a better time than now to start your own business. Apart from the redundancy money, which some lucky people get in large quantities, giving them a head start, there is (just as important) the free or heavily subsidised or grant-aided training programme which the Government and Local Authorities are falling over themselves to provide. Use these as much as you like. Exploit them for all you're worth. Take advantage of every training course in sight, every apprenticeship workshop that's offered. Don't be too proud to work a few weeks or a few months for almost nothing just to learn the trade. (It's the trade and skill that matters not the money – as we've all learned lately to our cost.)

The jobs listed here are practical, down-to-earth, nothing fanciful, silly or hard to get. (The Silly Season is over now . . . perhaps for all of our lifetime.) However, you may notice after a glance at the list at the beginning, a number of jobs here which you might think of as, say, borderline – between what you'd like and what the Authorities allow! I beg you not to let this put you off. I envisage for the future a much more flexible society, where responsible citizens will make more and more of their own decisions. (Like running a private postal service in your small town, for example – though I didn't actually dare to include this one or anything quite so daring!) But I foresee a society at least as flexible and independent as in the last century when you could open a school, start a hackney carriage business, begin a dancing class for young ladies: sell anything you like on the open market – anything that is, within reason. I do *not* mean a free-for-all as it sometimes was then, with crafty traders selling home-made hair restorer made of nothing. Strict Laws and Regulations, yes! Childish out-of-date interference from the Town Hall, no! And after all, nowadays we do have something called Consumer Protection, even if there are always people too lazy to use it.

In fact, the big new change to the more flexible society has already begun. Turn to page for example, and read the extraordinary concessions granted by the Minister of Transport to make better, more sensible use of your car in future. And look at the new financial benefits offered by Local Authorities (Surrey, Middlesex and elsewhere) for kind-hearted people with a good home to offer a convalescent holiday for patients discharged from hospital, thereby easing the burden on hard-pressed Health Service Staff.

Now . . . as to the jobs described in this book, I have given the name and address in each case of at least one Authority or Expert to whom you should apply before finally deciding which kind of work you will choose.

Among them are a number of success stories. Many of these people whom I interviewed when compiling the first edition of 'Making money at home' were visited by me again to see (a) if they were still in business and (b) whether they were prospering. The answer was 'yes' to both questions. (I do admit there were just a few who had not done well lately. Please avoid anything to do with fur or feathers, artificial flowers or cheap jewellery . . . all, alas, sadly out of fashion.) During the difficult period while you are making up your mind, you may have the misfortune to meet a certain kind of person who will want for your own sake, to give advice. This is the person (and they include those with experience and more, much more often, those without) who – no matter what you decide – will always be eager to tell you in the greatest detail, how it *cannot* be done.

Such persons are death to any

business, any effort, any love affair, any marriage or faith. My advice is to listen to what they have to say, but make up your own mind!

Remember . . . that although you should start small you are going to be in-pocket right away because you have stopped commuting. The maddest commuters are, of course, in South-East England (where I used to be one of them myself), carted about like tormented cattle at a hugely inflated price. They commute daily to work from Margate to London; from Ipswich to Birmingham; from Chester to Manchester; from Whitley Bay to Newcastle and even Glasgow . . . from all expensive points of the compass. Even short-run commuters, say 20-miles from London are quids-in by working at home. They start by saving £15 to £20 a week simply by *not* commuting. Add to that the cost of bad meals eaten out, of catching the 'flu several times a winter from overheated or freezing trains. In the Britain which I foresee there will be few unhappy commuters. All facilities will be on tap in much the same way they were when I was a small child growing up in Birmingham . . . where the Dress-maker, Shirtmaker, Doctor, Dentist, Schoolhouse, Sunday School, Piano-tuner, Homebaker, Wireless-set Maker, Curtain Maker, Watchmaker, etc., were all to be found either in our road or just around the corner. Rather a quiet road it was. With trees. Most of the residents had a little front garden, a bit of lawn and flowerbeds. Inside those houses there was not only a private life, with lots of children, but there was almost always a private business too where people felt secure despite the big Depression, because they were Making enough Money at Home.

# The jobs

Alterations and repairs
Antique dealer
Artist
Auctioneer's porter

Beautician and beauty therapist
Beekeeper

Caterer for parties
Cat's home or cattery
Chartered Accountant
Chicken farmer
Childbirth (Nat. Childbirth Trust
   Lecturer)
China repairer
Chiropodist
Cleaner and spring-cleaner
Computer programmer
Confectioner
Corsetiere
Craft Worker

Dance Teacher
Doll restorer
Dressmaker
Driving instructor

English Teacher
Envelope addresser

Flower arranger and florist
Foster parent
French polisher

Gardener
Genealogist
Goat-keeper

Hairdresser
Home economist
Home shopper
Host Family (1 & 2)
Housewife's shopping driver

Indexer

Journalist
Junk restorer

Kleeneze salesperson
Knitter

Lampshade maker
Leather worker
Lip-reading teacher

Marriage bureau
Mother's help
Montessori teacher
Motorcar repairer
Mushroom grower
Music teacher

Nurse

Odd jobs

Patchwork quilt maker
Photographer
Pippa-Dee party giver
Potter
Pre-school playgroup organiser

Rabbit farmer
Researcher and social survey
   interviewer
Room-letter

Servicemaster's assistant

Teas and refreshments
Tourist's guide and escort
Telephone salesperson
Toy maker
Translator
Tupperware party hostess
Tutoring
Typist

Upholsterer

Windowcleaner
Writer

Yoga teacher

# How to use this book

The first chapter contains in alphabetical order a list of jobs to attract and inspire you; it is not comprehensive – but it gives an idea of what can be done. Each job carries a detailed list of guidance, but as things change so rapidly you must be prepared to make some investigations of your own. I've done the basics for you! Remember, when you write to people and organisations, that a large self-addressed stamped envelope will often help to get a prompt reply. *This is important.*

The second chapter is planned to start you on the homework you've got to do before you start; it introduces you to two women, Ann and Kate, who've 'done it all' and will put you in the picture on various questions you should consider at the outset. This is the 'how to set about it stage', and the chapter continues with a section advising on Business or Office Technique to impress on you the importance of keeping orderly notes and files; so that, whether you employ an accountant to help you or not, you will have all your business affairs in order. Then follows, in this same chapter, the three stages of: Organising; Finance; Law. Included in this chapter is a piece I've called 'Tax Extra' which presents a few homely words of advice about how to keep the income-tax man happy. Believe me, it's just like a marriage; if you keep him happy, you'll be happy too! This chapter ends with advice on legal problems (which you should study carefully).

The third chapter contains a few slightly bitter comments from me about how *not* to make a telephone call; and more positive tips on how to use a business letter. A list of useful contacts follows, including some addresses you could need which are mentioned in other parts of the book. The book ends with a complete index to make it easy for you to find what you want under the job you have chosen. All addresses and phone numbers are bang-up-to-date at the time of printing.

There is every incentive for you to start going into business immediately – quite apart from your need for money! Recurring economic crises mean that many essential jobs are vacant because for one thing, Local Authorities nowadays just do not have the money to provide services they formerly did. It's up to you to try and fill in some of these gaps. Those, obviously, include the homelier tasks like home-helps, window-cleaners, and so on, but you will find that the list of jobs in Chapter I includes every kind of work possible, artistic, creative, intellectual, socially worthy and some new and unusual ones.

This book is not written and planned with women only in mind. Most of the tasks listed are jobs which men also do.

**Important:** I have covered in the relevant sections various bye-laws and restrictions on working at home. Acquaint yourself with the rules and, wherever possible, try to conform but never, never allow yourself to be bullied or intimidated either by the rules themselves or by anyone who tries to alarm you with them. Some of the rules – especially those relating to food and hygiene – are sensible; stick to them. Do not break the law but, on the other hand, do not make a fool of yourself either. Some of the rules are often slightly out-dated or even slightly potty. Like asking you to buy yourself a bottle sterilising machine for your kitchen as though you were a full-blown dairy farmer and a printing press to have your name printed on the bottles! Sure . . . you'll buy the lot and several washing-machines thrown in; when you're rich as rich, if that'll keep the Council happy. Like hell you will! You are expected to try and keep the rules where possible; you are *not* expected to go quite mad doing it.

In any case, many of the rules can be obeyed in a much better way by deciding (where food is concerned) to work under the auspices of that splendid body the National Federation of Women's Institutes. (You will find all this explained in the Section on Law.)

In this way you can avoid all that to-ing and fro-ing with your local Town Hall. Some people get confused about the difference between being self-employed and starting your own business.

For the former you need no one's permission, though you should pay your own National Insurance and get your card stamped each week (or month) at the Post Office.

For the latter you should register your company, and if you plan to employ someone you must inform the Department of Employment. Hence this book to explain the rules. Finally, a word about morale. Please try and choose one of the jobs which you enjoy because that's good for morale. Morale is what you need to become a successful Armchair Capitalist. Good Luck!

*Part One*

# Jobs to attract and inspire you

## Alterations and Repairs  *M/F  17–70*

### (Also amateur dramatic society costumier)

Almost no investment needed, if you have your own sewing machine. Modest, steady to good income. Can be done at home. (See also *Dressmaking*, page 28.)

**Qualifications and training**
Ability to sew.
Train with sewing lessons at evening classes, or for a special short course in dressmaking try the School of Dressmaking and Design, 69 Wells Street London W1 (Tel: 01-580-9018). Also try your technical college or university or London Education Authority.

**Equipment**
Sewing machine (secondhand prices range from £25 to £70) shears etc. Customers supply their own materials, patterns and extras.

**Helpers**
Some women friends who can also sew and who will work for you when necessary. For example local Amateur Dramatic Societies are always looking for someone to make the clothes for a whole show. (You can if you wish, keep the clothes and hire them out again.)
I know one woman in a country town who was formerly a sewing-teacher to handicapped people and now makes a living from alterations only. She has a friend who is an excellent cutter, and farms out the sewing to local people, selling the finished garments to local boutiques.

**Premises**
Your own room at home.

**Write to**
Your nearest Amateur Dramatic Society and ask if they would like your services dressing their new show.

**Law**
No restrictions.

**Advertising**
Work up a market by personal contact and recommendation. Put a small notice in a shop window. Also ask the local boutique or clothing store to recommend you. Do not forget to ask the local (couturier-trained) dressmaker to recommend you also. Full-time dressmakers hate doing alterations.

**What you can earn**
My friend had no idea what to charge for her work. So she simply made an hourly charge of £2 but you can make your own price and arrangements.
Current commercial charges range from £3.50 to shorten a skirt; £4 if flared; repair of pockets, minimum £2.10 each; making up a dress £6.50; dress and jacket £8.50. Charge about 50p per hour for repairs, alterations, hems etc and more for a specialist job like smocking and embroidery.

3

**Advantages**
You can work when you feel like it without losing the time on fittings and appointments that a dressmaker does.

**Disadvantages**
You will not get rich doing alterations; but if you could add some part-time dressmaking – for the Local Amateur Dramatic Society – this could be profitable and adds variety. You've got to learn to go metric!

## *Antique Dealer* M/F 15–55

Investment can be very high or very low depending on the kind of business. Income can be very high or intermittent depending on how many hours or days you can work. Can be done at home, or from home or at a local street market, depending on how far you want to travel.

If you decide to specialise, say, in antique dolls – currently fashionable – you can work entirely at home, restoring and mending, and above all *exhibiting* your own 'collection'.

**Qualifications**
There are two types of business:

1) The amateur who hires a stall for a few pounds a day or half-a-day in any public market, e.g. Petticoat Lane, Portobello Road in London, at any country market throughout Britain, or at any of the hundreds of Sunday markets in the UK (which you find advertised in local papers).

2) Top class antique dealing, which requires membership of the British Antique Dealers' Association, or membership of a similar professional body in the Art World.

Qualifications for No. 1 should include some knowledge and a great deal of enthusiasm.

Qualifications for No. 2 are as follows:– You should have been established in business on your own account in the antique trade for a period of not less than three years, possess the necessary knowledge to enable you to buy or sell goods of the kind in which you normally deal; carry a stock of articles not less than 100 years old, kept separately from more recent items;

carry on business from premises open to the public; be proposed and seconded for membership of the British Antique Dealers' Association. Entrance fee is £75, annual subscription of £125 is payable on election and this includes a Certificate of Membership; and hanging Signs, Window Tablets, Fair Emblems and blocks can be bought from them. (The most important condition is the first one, i.e. to be in the business for three years.)

**Training**
The best way to train to enter the No. 2 business is to start work in the No. 1; or you can take a Diploma course at West Dean College, Sussex University in the restoration of antique furniture and antique clocks. These diplomas are now recognised by the National Trust and the Victoria and Albert Museum. Taking a stall requires no training of any kind. (I did it myself several times, for the *Daily Mail* and the *Evening Standard*) in order to write articles on what it's like to hire a £5 stall for the day in Petticoat Lane (it now costs more than double this) and flog a lot of supposedly 'antique' British rubbish. I am ashamed to say I made £50 out of a stall of rubbish, battered bellows and fire irons, bits of marcasite and fake jewellery, ancient paintings and a decrepit half-ruined chaise longue.) Browse around the antique shops in small country towns and markets every weekend until you recognise what is good and what has value and what sells. Read also reference books for silver and china and learn their

4

marks and their values. Ask questions of experienced dealers.

## Equipment

For Business No. 1 you can probably start with oddments from your own attic (if you have an attic). You also need between £6 and £12 to hire a stall somewhere, and enough money (if you haven't a car) to transport you to the stall at the market which may possibly open between 6.00 and 8.00 a.m. Brighton: A stall for Saturday 8 a.m. to 1 p.m. costs £6 to £7. Portobello Road: A whole day costs £10 to £12.

For Business No. 2, obviously you need at least £1000 to start buying one or two genuine antiques.

## Premises

No. 1: a stall. No. 2: you can do this in a discreet way in your own home. It helps to live in a stylish kind of a house or better still, in an old house which has been refurbished and redecorated to make it a good foil for some of your antiques, but this is not essential or even strictly necessary. Your own private background really doesn't matter. It could be a caravan or a costly house in the suburbs. As your business develops, however, you will be able to keep your antiques on your own sideboard or walls until the time comes for a local market to open.

For Business No. 1, you may need extra storage space; a garage, loft or attic, where you can store the bargains you buy ready to pile on your stall in the market.

## Write to

The Secretary of BADA (British Antique Dealers' Association Ltd), 20 Rutland Gate, London SW7 1BD (Tel: 01-589 4128/2102). BADA publish a journal for private circulation to members.

Business No. 1; Study the morning and evening newspapers in your town and the advertisement hoardings to make a note of market days and opening times. The advertisements should give the names and telephone number of the Market Superintendent or Organiser. Book your stand in advance if possible; otherwise get up very early or you will find there is a queue and no room for your stall or you've been squeezed out into the rain or into a bad position.

## Law

Get in touch with the C.A.B., about consulting a lawyer on how to avoid the various pitfalls awaiting the unwary beginner in this trade. For instance, there has been a large increase in art thefts since the war. Persuade an established art and antique dealer to explain the niceties of keeping on the right side of the law and how to protect yourself against phoney antiques and phoney anything.

## Advertising

In the normal channels, newspapers, newsagents, trade journals, by exhibition locally or at antique fairs.

## What you can earn

The pickings are enormous in this trade, but to achieve a reasonable income requires knowledge and expertise and competition amongst dealers is pretty cut-throat. (You may have the skill and art knowledge to become another Duveen, the famous art dealer whose amusing biography can be found in most libraries.) However, in the somewhat down-at-heel open market business, you can make a substantial weeky income if you can spare one day (or better still two days) a week standing in an open market in all weathers, flogging lamps, lampshades, leather belts, old books etc. Do not be too shy to ask advice from neighbouring stallholders. Many take a pride and pleasure in being genuinely helpful – as long as you are not exhibiting the same type of goods.

## Advantages

It's exciting – especially to people interested in the world of Arthur Negus. (He once told me in an interview that whenever he gets home after a few days away, he finds his garage is full of articles people have left inside with little notes attached asking 'is this really old?')

**Disadvantages**
You need money to be successful in No. 2. In No. 1 – well it's draughty in Petticoat Lane at 6 o'clock on a Sunday Morning.

## Artist   M/F   18–80

*(Painting, caricature, cartoons, oils, water colours, also TV graphics, newspaper graphic drawings, business letter heads, commercial design posters, book jackets, painting child portraits from 'snaps' etc.)*

Investment can be high but high income also. Can be done at home.

**Qualifications and Training**
Talent is essential.
Train at an academy or school of art; at any part-time or evening art class; at an Adult Education College; on regular holidays with an art class and tutor. Constant practice is necessary; visit art galleries and exhibitions. Consult an organisation called AIR, for advice. This is the Art Information Registry; it has its own gallery in London at 125/129 Shaftesbury Avenue, London WC2H 8AD (Tel: 01-240 3149) and holds exhibitions at two-to-three-week intervals.

**Equipment**
Paints, easels, brushes etc. Try for some secondhand materials from art shops. You need designers' colours, lay out paper, sheets of good paper 5" × 7" at 6p a sheet, a box of Rotring pens, and if possible an air brush, camera etc., and a 'T' square for lining up your paper to see if its straight. (Instead of buying trays for your photo-negatives costing £3 each, buy from Boots some cat litter trays at 40p each.)

**Premises**
Ideally a studio at home, with plenty of light and space. Plus angle-poise tilted drawing board, about £10 new.

**Write to**
AIR (see above). Try to find (in your local library) their booklet called 'Airmail' which is now out of print; you can consult it at AIR's Offices. (This gives all possible information for anyone interested in the arts; names and addresses of societies and clubs concerned with architecture, design, film, music, poetry and the visual arts; also has information on grants, awards, exhibitions, festivals, scholarships, jobs, art centres, galleries, museums, studios, workshops, materials equipment etc.)

Also . . . to an organisation called 'Space' which supplies studios to painters, sculptors etc., at a reasonable rent! For their address, ask the Arts Council, London, the Greater London Arts Association, c/o the GLC, County Hall, London SW1, who can also advise on provincial art centres.

More information on studios, galleries and artists, consult the 'Directory of Artists'. This costs £2 from AIR, Shaftesbury Avenue (see above) or £1.50 if you can call in for it.

**Law**
No restrictions, unless you're Tom Keating!

**Advertising**
Your own exhibition is best.

**What you can earn**
Prices range from about £12 to £150 or more per work of art, depending on your talent. AIR takes 10% commission if they handle your work. Very high income if any TV company or commercial firm takes a fancy to one of your designs, a successful business letter head design, for example.

**Advantages**
You can keep your artist's smock on while you do the washing up (which saves time). Apart from the hope of money and fame – painting is the newest medical cure for neurosis or unhappiness.

**Disadvantages**
You may have to pay for your models! More still if they are nude.

**Note:**
Although caricatures and cartoons are included in this section for training and study, the actual marketing of such work really belongs under journalism. Therefore study that section (page 48) for general advice because a similar approach to newspapers and magazines applies, except that the caricaturist or cartoonist should approach the Art Editor or Picture Editor first to get advice and to show samples of his or her work. (Unlike the reporter, the cartoonist must always take samples of his work with him when calling on various journals.)

The quality papers would pay lower fees (for a beginner perhaps as little as £12) than the mass circulation papers and magazines because there would be a certain 'prestige value' for an unknown artist in getting a cartoon published. This might even lead to an offer of a staff job (which could be done from a studio at home) from any Editor who happened to see it.

---

## *Auctioneer's Porter* M/F 16–40

---

No Investment. Small earner although this means working a few hours each day AWAY from home, I am including this job and a few others (see Cleaner, Driving Instructor etc.) because it could lead to better things. Example: by doing this job for a few weeks or months, you would gain valuable knowledge (for free) about antiques, pictures, china, furniture to qualify you for better work; (see page 4, *Antique Dealer*). Duties consist of helping to carry in furniture, bric-à-brac, linen bundles, blankets, anything to be included in the current sale; help to arrange the small antique items, jewellery, vases, glass, ceramics, clocks, watches in large glass cases; help to catalogue and number all items, arrange the seating for the public on sale day; be ready on sale day to stand by the rostrum in order to display items as called by the Auctioneer. After the sale help to pack up sold items and if possible, to assist in carrying out to customer's transport if not too heavy. This may seem a lot of work but it only lasts the three or four days of viewing and the actual day of the sale.

**Qualifications**
Health and Strength.

**Training**
You train while you work.

**How to Train**
Apply for work at your nearest auctioneer's office or large furniture store.

**Equipment**
Your own overall unless one is provided.

**Premises**
Outside your home.

**Write to**
Any auctioneer's address you see either advertised locally or in newspapers.

**Law**
No restrictions.

**Advertising**
Cards in newsagents windows.

**What you earn**
£1.00 per hour; it is listed as casual labour.

**Advantages**
As stated above, this is one of those jobs which you should try to use as your 'University' to get knowledge you would otherwise have to pay for at a College of Education or Evening Class.

---

## Beautician    F    16–150

### (and/or beauty counsellor)

Investment can be small if you work for a large firm or high if you buy all the equipment available. Income can be good to very good. Can be done at home or on visits to clients in their homes.

### Qualifications and Training
A beautician is a beauty therapist and must be qualified. A beauty Counsellor can give simple treatments like manicure or shampoo but her job mainly is to advise generally about cosmetics.

To qualify as a beautician or Beauty Therapist, training and a diploma course in at least some of the following are essential; beauty therapy and cosmetics, body massage, hair grooming, bust treatments, slimming techniques, electrolysis and wax depilation, speciality facials, cosmetic chemistry, fashion make-up, eyelash tinting, skin treatments.

There are a number of courses; some are expensive; some at local Authority education centres are less so. However, if you plan to work at home on your own, without the backing of one of the larger firms, then you should train and take one or more of the diploma courses offered. The diplomas can be exhibited in your home.

The London College of Fashion, 20 John Prince's Street, London W1M 9HE (Tel: 01-629 9401/9412) has a helpful course in their Department of Hairdressing and Beauty Therapy. They offer a special 3-year Diploma Course which combines hairdressing and beauty therapy (thereby amalgamating two separate 2-year courses). Some courses are full-time and others are part-time but they cannot be done by post. (Fees are £170 p.a. and there is no fee for those under 18 years of age.) This course provides tuition in hairdressing and wig making with the full range of beauty therapy studies and also lessons in anatomy, physiology, hygiene, first aid, nutrition, cosmetics science, business studies and so on.

To enrol, you must be over 16 and have a minimum of 5 passes at GCE 'O' level or the equivalent including English and a Science subject. Some of the courses are for girls only. The course is very popular so applications should be made at least a year in advance. You could get a grant, or a reduced fee, or have your employer pay for the course. *BUT* . . . for Beauty Counselling, try one of the well known cosmetic manufacturers near you, where training is free or not very expensive.

## Equipment
This can include such expensive items as electrolysis equipment and/or a fully equipped trolley for complete manicures and pedicures. Try for secondhand equipment. The cost of your equipment will, however, depend on whatever speciality you choose. If you specialise in facials and Beauty Treatments, you might be able to avoid high investment by representing one of the larger cosmetic makers like Max Factor, Yardley or a similar firm.

## Premises
You will need an attractive, hygienic properly equipped room to give confidence to clients; also a waiting room if possible.

## Write to
To qualify as a fully-fledged beautician, ask your Local Authority to suggest education and training on the lines of above.

## Qualifications and Training
Your area or the nearest big town should have similar courses.

To qualify as a Beauty Counsellor write to some of the important cosmetic firms.

For advice on high earning Beauty Therapy write to the Christine Shaw Company, 11 Old Bond Street, Mayfair, London W1X 3DB (Tel: 01-629 3884/3885 (24 hours)). They run a Presentation One Year Diploma Course in Beauty and a five-month Course in other beauty treatments. These are rather classy affairs costing a lot of money, especially if you take all the courses.

## Law
Remember that all private practitioners of beauty or hairdressing etc., run a risk, however careful and meticulous you may be, of causing some injury to a patient (for example, despite careful testing beforehand, a patient may still prove to be allergic in some way to a new shampoo or skin treatment). Therefore, if you are not protected by membership of a professional body, then consult an insurance company and take out a separate policy against such an unhappy incident. This should cover both yourself and your client.

## Advertising
In magazines such as *Vogue, Woman's Journal, Woman* or *Woman's Own*. Or locally through your hairdresser. For advertising electrolysis treatment, you may need sponsorship or permission from your Local Authority.

## What you can earn
This varies considerably, according to your district, your clientele, your own diplomas or lack of them, and what you offer.

## Advantages
A good idea is to work up a 'practice' offering a local service. For example, you could offer 'specials' like pre-wedding make-up. This work appeals to many women of any age and, through recommendation, it is possible to build up a paying business – without losing your own looks!

## Disadvantages
Some home-based women do not want to live in an all-woman world. A mixed sex clientele is unusual, as statistics show that few men respond to this sort of selling. Mobility, essential for door to door selling, can involve further expense.

Low investment. Small but steady income. Can be done at home in your own garden. If you live in a town suburb and have a flourishing garden, you can keep bees provided you are fully experienced and knowledgeable.

## Qualifications

Read and thoroughly digest the advice in as many books on beekeeping as you can find in your library. Consult the British Beekeepers' Association before you start.

## Training

Some people learn the hard way by getting the bees before the books. The books should come first.

The Association says: 'Beekeeping is an ancient craft now modernised with close associations with husbandry generally.' They insist this means you ought to swot up knowledge of genetics, anatomy, pathology and animal behaviour. They recommend the following books as 'required reading':

*Preliminary stage*
1. Butler, C. G., *Beekeeping* – Min. of Agriculture Bulletin No. 9.
2. Hamilton, W., *The Art of Beekeeping* – York Herald Printing Works.

*Intermediate stage*
1. Butler, C. G., *The World of the Honeybee* – Collins.
2. *Swarming of Bees* – Min. of Agriculture Bulletin No. 206.
3. *Flowers Month by Month* – Bee Research Association. (All the books mentioned above should be available in your local library).

*Senior stage*
1. Berry, R. J., *Teach yourself genetics* – English University Press.
2. Bailey, L., *Infectious Diseases of the Honeybee* – Land Books Limited. (Obtainable on loan from County Libraries and County Beekeeping Associations.) Also get free beginner's leaflets from the Ministry of Agriculture Publications Department, Tolcarne Drive, Pinner, Middlesex, or get free bulletins from any good bookstall, Nos 9, 100 and 206.

## Equipment

You can buy a 'Beginner's Kit' which costs about £125 and does not include bees. Or make your own for say £80.

## Premises

You do need a garden big enough, so you can keep the bees well away from the house. Bees should have access to pollen within a certain radius. This varies according to the locality. Consult B.B.A.

## Write to

The Secretary of the British Beekeeper's Association, (Mr G. W. Knights, 28 Argyle Street, Reading, Berks RG1 74P) enclosing a stamped, self-addressed envelope, and he will put you in touch with your local Association. Or try National Agriculture Centre, Stoneleigh, Warwickshire.

## Law

Consult B.B.A. regarding bye-laws as they vary according to district (or the nearness of your nearest neighbour!)

Small investment, good steady income. Can be done at home.

### Qualifications
Best of course is for you to have at some time owned a bicycle of your own, even if it was years ago!

### Training
Go and watch someone doing it; ask questions and take notes. Read books with simple diagrams. Any of these books would teach you:
1. Bursty, B., *Bicycle Repair and Maintenance* (Avco, N.Y.) £1.75.
2. Sams, H. W., *Bicycle Maintenance and Repair* (U.S.) 70p.
3. *Brakes, Chains and Derailleurs* 70p.
4. *Frames, Tyres and Wheels*, £2.50.
5. Watson, Gray Martin, R., *The Penguin Book of the Bicycle* (Allen Lane) £5.50; (Penguin) £1.95.
6. *Fix Your Bicycle – all speeds, all major makes – Simplified Step by Step* £2. Clymer Publications, U.S.
7. *Bicycles* (Consumer Research) (Longmans) 80p.
8. *Bicycles. How to ride and maintain them.* Diana Gribble and Hilary McPhee. (Kestrel Books) £1.20. (Penguin) 60p.
   Also Halfords do their own book obtainable at any Halfords Shop.
   For specialist equipment, cycle trailers etc., try the Kensington Cycle Co., Kensington Student Centre, Kensington Church Street, London W8 or Bike Hod Ltd., 45 Charlotte Road, London EC2A 3PD. Send S.A.E. for their leaflet.

### Equipment
Lots of spanners, various sizes, adjustable spanner, pliers, oil, soldering kit, tyre levers, puncture outfits (rubber cement and patches may be bought in bulk – ask your local bike shop). Padlock, spare lamps (a bike is now a valuable piece of property, new worth £60 minimum.

### Premises
A garden shed is a help. Your front or back garden. Or a piece of yard outside your home. Your front porch. Tarpaulin for bad weather.

### Write to
Everyone you know, friends, schools, the Post Office. (Remember that in the past two decades, pedal cycles went out of fashion, so that bicycle shops, cycle dealers and above all, bicycle repairers are nowhere to be found. Since the oil crisis and the Recession, people who were lucky enough to have kept their old bikes have had a terrible struggle to find someone to repair them.

### What you can earn
You must charge for materials plus time. Never separate these on the bill; put it all together. It is a good idea to sell second-hand bikes as well (if you can get hold of any!) . . . persuade people to sell their old ones for a small sum; then renovate and sell them.
So you *must* show where you are to be found.)

### Law
You don't have to bother about it! But it helps for you to learn the Road Safety Laws for cars and lorries; so you know what to avoid.

### Advertising
Ads in papers; cards in newsagents' windows.

### Advantages
No shortage of customers nowadays.

### Disadvantages
You'll be tempted to sell your own bike, but DON'T!

# Book-Keeping  M/F  18–70

Small investment or none. Good income for steady, regular work. Can be done at home.

## Qualifications
If you are good at maths, you could probably qualify by doing a Home Study Course (see Useful Contacts for a Correspondence College). Most people either do a term at evening classes or several terms and take a final exam: or they pick up a basis for further study while working as a junior typist or secretary.

## Training
You could take a secretarial course which includes basic book-keeping. This includes Book-keeping Stage I in a part-time or full-time course. Try the City of London Polytechnic, Moorgate, London EC2, evening class for intermediate and final courses. There are 29 colleges and Polys in the London area alone giving a part-time book-keeping day class. For other parts of the U.K. consult your local Education Department.

## How to Train
If you have a basic knowledge of how to keep books, from working in a shop or office, you can learn the rest as you go along, because most firms have their own methods and would perhaps prefer to teach you themselves.

## Equipment
Pocket calculator (new) costs from £1.66 to £20.11 and secondhand up to £8.50. You would use the firm's adding machine, but you could get a secondhand one for about £35 or a new electric one for £100.

## Premises
A table in a quiet room at home, and a cupboard that you can lock up when you leave the room; you must remember that the book-keeping documents entrusted to you are confidential and must be kept entirely safe!

## Write to
As you want to work at home, this is a case where the best idea is to call rather than write. Visit your local tradesmen (the butcher, baker, candlestick maker, etc,) small shops, local farmers, hairdressers in your neighbourhood. Be prepared to offer references.

## Law
No restrictions.

## Advertising
No restrictions. You can put 'ads' about yourself in newspapers under 'Business Services' or in newsagents' windows.

## What you can earn
You can charge by the hour roughly what a fully qualified secretary would charge. You must charge for your travel expenses by bus or car if you have to collect and deliver the books yourself.

## Advantages
It is work perhaps most readily available to you nowadays and it can lead to regular business.

## Disadvantages
There is a rush of work at particular times of the week or month, when you may feel overworked.

No investment strictly necessary. Very high income. Can be done mainly at home.

## Qualifications
No special qualifications or training needed, except a talent for cooking and the domestic arts.

## Training
A domestic science course at evening class or a specialist course such as Cordon Bleu school provides.

## How to train
If you can cook, then you can train yourself by studying any good cookery book. I suggest the best kind of training for this job is to try out new recipes on your own family and at your own parties and ask for reactions.

## Equipment
Ideally, you need in your own kitchen: a good size oven, refrigerator, freezer, (though this is a luxury item and you can manage without it), an electric blender and mixer if possible, plenty of working space in the kitchen, good baking-tins, pans and ovenware, pastry shapes, tools for making fancy cream filling, as well as essential cookery tools, wooden spoons, beaters, sharp kitchen knives etc. A good supply of containers with sealing tops (Tupperware) etc and lots of silver foil. Ideally, your own motor car for transport. White overall or pinafore (for those occasions where you stay on at the party and help with the serving).

Don't forget to take out a separate small insurance policy against possible damage to one of your 'party' customers.

## Premises
If you have no freezer, then plenty of good, cool larder space. Your own kitchen at home is the best possible place for this job. Failing this, ask if you can use a friend's or neighbour's kitchen (even if your kitchen is rather small you can still do this job because you can prepare a day or two in advance).

## Write to
See paragraph below on the law. Contact your Local Council (Planning Officer, Environmental Health Officer) unless you are a member of the W.I., in which case ask their advice re: law.

## Law
The laws are strict on food hygiene if you are selling food to the public. If you are a member of the W.I., they will take care of this legal side of it for you. Otherwise consult your Local Authority, who will advise you. Buy a copy of the Food Hygiene (General) Regulations 1970 (No. S.I. 1970 No. 1172) from H.M.S.O. (see useful contacts) or through any bookseller.

## Advertising
A card in the newsagents' window. Advertisements in your local evening paper. I interviewed a number of women in the south-east who are doing excellent business catering for fork suppers for between 30–40 people at a time; weddings, birthdays, anniversaries. In one case, two housewives joined forces and have more orders than they can manage. They make vol-au-vents or exotic hors d'oeuvres, a hot main dish and an elaborate sweet, then they put everything back into containers, stack it in the car and drive it to the party (sometimes staying to serve but normally remaining in the kitchen so that the hostess can claim she did it all by herself!)

## What you can earn
Naturally depends on what you give the customers to eat, but the ladies mentioned above charge £5.50 per head. If you do this job inside the

London area and provide top class food, you can charge £7.50 per head and upwards.

**Advantages**
You can meet a lot of interesting people. It is interesting, creative work. Apart from the shopping, it is all done in your own home. The two women referred to above each have three children under twelve years of age whom they leave with their husbands if it's an evening party. However, they were soon making enough money to pay for qualified babysitters or nannies.

This is a business which remains more or less unaffected by economic crisis. Parties, weddings and birthdays are something that go on and on, even during a depression, winter and summer, autumn and spring.

**Disadvantages**
The only one (and I had to be told about this) is that business can become so booming, you don't have time to give birthday parties for your own children or husbands. The two Kent housewives mentioned above told me recently: 'since you interviewed us four years ago, we've got rich!'

## Cat's Hotel-Keeper M/F 20–55

Fair but not too high investment. Fair income from boarding; very low from breeding. Can be done at home (not necessarily in the house!)

**Qualifications and training**
A love for and knowledge of cats. A willingness to be tied to them and to your home. Cat care is important because you need some veterinary knowledge. If you don't know how to care for cats, all your profits will go on vet's bills! Cats can get 'flu or gastro-enteritis for which they need injections. Visit cat shows and talk to experts. Get full information from members of the Governing Council of the Cat Fancy.

**Equipment**
If you decide to run a Cattery or Cat Boardinghouse, you will need a well equipped cat-house with cat kennels, properly heated and with electric light. (You'll also need gloves as protection against cats who may scratch, and to wear when opening the cages to feed them.)
For cat breeding: no permission, no special premises required. More than 40–50 cats is frowned upon by the F.A.B. as an overcrowded Cattery; each council levies its own fee, ranging from

£8 to £10, £20 or £30. Write for advice to Mrs Alison Ashford, Annelida, Roundwell, Bearsted, Maidstone, Kent (Tel: Maidstone (0622) 37050). You are advised to keep breeding separate from boarding to avoid cross-infection.

**Premises**
For your Cattery, possibly a large summer-house in the garden would do for a small-scale business. However, to run a Cattery on commercial lines, you need a large, well-constructed shed.

**Write to**
For advice on catteries, Miss S. M. Hamilton-Moore of the Feline Advisory Bureau, Cats' Hotel, Orcheston, Nr. Salisbury, Wilts. (Enclose postal order for £2 plus 18p P & P.)

**Law**
You will need a licence from your Local Authority to run a Cattery or a Cat Boardinghouse. Check on required cage size with neighbouring authorities as well as your own.

**Advertising**
Advertise where you like: local and national papers, specialist magazines. You may well receive orders from

abroad (consult the Feline Advisory Bureau about quarantine regulations); export business like this will help you with your income-tax returns.

**What you can earn**
A Cattery with, say, 70 or 80 cats (see above comment on over-crowding) can be a big earner: for accommodation with full board, fix your price according to the facilities you offer. (It is probably a good idea to see what other people charge for what.)

**Advantages**
If you're a cat-lover, it won't feel like hard work.

**Disadvantages**
If you're not so passionate about them, it will. You have to stay at home 24 hours a day every day of the year or employ someone to supervise in your absence.

**Warning**
The F.A.B. warn there is no big money to be made but in the case of, say, a husband and wife team where husband has some employment or adequate pension, an adequate living can be made by the people if the Cattery is properly run.

---

## Chartered Accountant M/F 18–65

---

High investment in terms of time and effort. Low investment when fully qualified. Income very good to high. Can be done at home or on visits to clients.

**Qualifications and training**
Good educational background. You must satisfy the general requirements for entry to the University or Polytechnic to which you apply, which is usually at least 6 G.C.E. passes including 2 at 'A' level or their equivalent.

A student must enter into a training contract with a practising Chartered Accountant who is authorised to train students. During this time you have to pass I.C.A. exams in Accountancy, Law, Economics, Statistics, Taxation, Auditing, Systems and Data Processing. Graduates who already hold a degree in any subject must train for three years and non-graduates for four years, after completion of a full-time Foundation Course of one year at an approved polytechnic. However, special conditions may apply for holders of overseas degrees or older students (e.g. married women who interrupted their careers) with relevant experience.

Students who enter into a full-time training contract with a practising Chartered Accountant can expect to be paid a modest wage from the start, increasing with experience. The Institute of Chartered Accountants produces two Directories of Training Opportunities for graduates and non-graduates, and a list of local accountancy career advisers who can assist a student to find a suitable firm. Alternatively, you can contact the District Society of Chartered Accountants in your area, which will have a list of such firms.

**Equipment**
This is minimal. Ledgers and cash books, files, pencils, pens. A calculating machine.

**Premises**
I quote from the guidance given me by the Student Counsellor of the Institute of Chartered Accountants in England and Wales, who says:
'A qualified Chartered Accountant stands a reasonably good chance of being able to work from home. Once qualified, many chartered accountants obtain work from home through personal contact, often working for the

firm with which they qualified.' So all you need is your own desk, book, files, table-lamp etc.

## Write to
The Student Counsellor of the Institute of Chartered Accountants in England, Wales and Scotland, P.O. Box 433, Chartered Accountants' Hall, Moorgate Place, London EC2P 2BJ (Tel: 01-628 7060). Scotland: write for advice to The School of Accountancy and Business Studies, 541 Argyle Street, Glasgow G2 8LW.

## Law
Many unqualified and semi-qualified accountants work at home regularly, this is perfectly legal. They often get work through agencies and they are qualified through their knowledge and experience of book-keeping and accountancy. There are no restrictions on accountancy work at home.

## Advertising
The Institute of Chartered Accountants in England, Wales and Scotland states categorically: 'It is not possible for a chartered accountant to advertise his or her services.' Nevertheless, any daily newspaper reveals a whole column of 'ads' offering Accountancy, Accounting Services, Book-keeping etc., so presumably these are non-members and not fully qualified.

## What you can earn
This varies considerably. Payment can be per hour, per day, per week or per job.

The Institute says:- 'Women chartered accountants receive equal pay with the men in the profession, and opportunities are excellent. The proportion of women entering each year has increased significantly – from 4% in 1967 to 12½% in 1974 – 22% in 1979, and is expected to continue to do so.

Once qualified, a woman has every chance of combining marriage, family and career, as there are excellent opportunities for working part-time or *even from home*. Membership of the Institute also ensures job flexibility and mobility, by supplying information on work opportunities in your local area.

## Advantages
There are Polytechnics and Colleges providing relevant courses in more than 25 towns and cities in Britain, and there are another 9 in the London area.

Local Education Authorities will normally give you a grant if you attend a foundation course.

## Disadvantages
Standards are pretty high; so even if you do have a good head for figures, it's not an easy choice – unless you are serious about having a top career and the intention to continue it at home.

Year ends can mean long hours and there will be dog days.

Some, if not most, work has to be done at client's offices.

---

## Chicken Farmer   M/F   18–65

---

Medium but not high investment. Modest, steady income. Can be done at home.

### Equipment and Premises
You do need suitable space for a chicken-run in your garden or yard, and room for their proper housing, one square foot per hen. You will need at least 12 hens to make any profit at all and you must sell over two dozen eggs a week to cover the cost of their feed.

The chicken-house and the feeding equipment and fencing is the most expensive part of the investment. You will require a chicken-house, feeding hoppers and troughs, drinking hoppers or troughs, fencing posts, heavy gauge wire and wire netting.

You will also require somewhere to store the feed.

*Housing:* Consult the Poultry Club on how to buy and select. Do not buy an expensive hen-house as advertised some years ago. (A new hen-house would cost £80 now.) See below.

*Fencing:* Decide how high this should be to be fox-proof; 6 ft. minimum and sunk below ground level.

*Free range:* Decide on how many birds and whether free-range or deep litter.

*Feed:* Mash mixed with cooked household scraps in morning or plain mash or pellets, 3–4 oz per bird depending on weight. Mixed corn afternoons, approximately a handful per bird.

*Selection:* Learn to select stock day-olds, 6-week old, point of lay. Anyone going into it as a business should not buy old birds.

Decide on what you want: hybrids for laying or pure bred or pure bred crossed. The lighter the bird generally, the more and smaller eggs – some are more suitable for free-range and some for more confined deep litter.

Buy secondhand housing with care and clean carefully and disinfect. Better to start new if cash available. Housing can be bought from Southern Pullet Rearers, 8 Fishbourne Road, Chichester, Sussex (Tel: Chichester (0243) 788551); also from Oakland Nurseries, High Tilt, Cranbrook, Kent (Tel: Cranbrook (0580) 713926). (Or if you are handy with wood, wire and tools you could easily build your own. Also install electric light.) Alternatively you could have a portable hen-house with wire run attached which you move up and down your lawn every day, saving a lot of mowing. However, moveable runs, while saving money on enclosed fencing do restrict the number of birds. The laying life of a hen is about three years; after that they will probably not pay their way and become more prone to disease. It is possible to vaccinate against various diseases, but it is also important to clean the houses out regularly. Always have young clean birds coming up to lay to ensure eggs over the moult period in the autumn.

You might decide not to buy pedigree hens, but to get them from a battery, where they are often sold off for about £1 each after a year to make way for new ones. (Pedigree hens are sold for about £2 each.)

You might also like to rear and fatten cockerels.

*More about feed:* Corn and meal are half the price at cash-and-carry than they are in pet shops, but it is better to have a local supplier.

## Write to

The General Secretary, Mrs Sue Hawkesworth, 24 Farris Barn Drive, Woodham, Weybridge, Surrey KT15 3DT (Tel: Byfleet (093 23) 46101). The annual subscription is now £6. For juniors under 16 and Old Age Pensioners it is £4. All members receive a free copy of the Poultry Club Year Book (which otherwise costs £2.25 inc. P & P). The Club also sends out quarterly newsletters and show bulletins giving details of forthcoming shows for people interested in exhibiting or attending shows, where stocks can be bought.

## Law

Ask your C.A.B. whether you have to inform the Local Authority. (You must bear in mind that the demands, tastes, preferences and bye-laws vary from one Local Authority to another.) There are strict laws relating to vaccination and relating to number of birds.

## What you can earn

A dozen farm eggs would now sell at around 75p. Persuade your regular customers to return the egg cartons: they're often in short supply and anyway it can eat into your profits.

## Advantages

You've always got something to eat in the house; you can make use of scraps;

chicken manure is excellent for the garden. Old hens can be sold for pie-making or soup.

**Disadvantages**
Chickens attract foxes and foxes can decimate a flock in one evening.

## Childbirth  F  25–45

### (National Childbirth Trust teacher)

No investment needed, but an annual fee of £6 is required to cover registration. Rock-bottom income. Can be done in your home or in neighbour's homes. (The fee should be sent with your application form to the Teachers' Panel Secretary at Headquarters – see below.) Annual fee for a (married) couple is £9. The same for overseas, inclusive of airmail postage.

This work is really only for young mothers of families, or for those hoping to start a family soon. The earnings from it are very small, usually only just enough to cover travelling expenses by car or bus from your home to neighbours or to the village hall or gymnasium or conference room. However, if you live in an area of young married couples, it is an interesting hobby, a means of meeting other young mums and above all an excellent preparation for your first or next child. You learn control and relaxation of your body and how to teach it to others.

#### Qualifications and training
Any teaching or other diploma but any well-adjusted, disciplined housewife can do it. Each trainee accepted by the Trust is required to sit in on two full courses of N.C.I. classes and to attend a weekend method seminar to learn the detailed principles of the method of preparation. Also to do a course of reading under a tutor's supervision. Full training may last one or two years of part-time work. Now you can have eight lessons at the headquarters for £21.30; for a couple the fee is £26.75. (At present the N.C.T. classes are organised only on a part-time basis). Finally you are required to write an essay of about 1500 words on a subject concerned with marriage, childbirth, emotions during pregnancy etc.

#### Equipment and Premises
When you are accepted as an N.C.T. teacher, you can take a class of women in your own home or wherever convenient.

#### Write to
The National Childbirth Trust, 9 Queensborough Terrace, London W2 3TB (Tel: 01-221 3833). (This is a registered charity.) It costs £6 annual subscription to be a member or £9 for a married couple.

#### What you can earn
The fee you can charge varies from about £2 a lesson, or barely enough to cover travel expenses. Organising classes in your own home with 12 to 15 women at a time can be more remunerative. Women who do this sort of work say that earnings really depend on how much time you can give.

#### Advantages
It's a great help to have all that knowledge when you're giving birth yourself.

#### Disadvantages
The low pay.

# China repairer  M/F  18–75

Low investment. Good income eventually. Can be done at home.

## Qualifications
You must attend classes to learn this craft. It could take three months to three years, depending on your ability.

## Training
There are many establishments throughout Britain teaching china mending – the repair and restoration of china and objets d'art. Also excellent classes run by Local Authorities.

## How to train
By attending courses such as those provided by Robin Hood's workshops, 18 Bourne Street, Sloane Square, London SW1 (Tel: 01-730 0425). They arrange them in sessions of 10 lessons, one each week for 10 weeks. Do remember to send a s.a.e. for details of classes. The school is unable to give advice by post.

The first five lessons teach the use of up-to-date materials and methods employed both commercially and by museums for taking apart old repairs and rebonding them and the filling and tinting of chips and cavities.

Advanced study follows in the next five lessons, such as the modelling of missing parts, taking impressions and castings, as well as instruction in the use of the electric hand drill and the air brush for spraying paint. The fee for a course like this is usually payable in advance – £60 plus VAT at the current rate = £69.

Local Authority classes are, of course, much cheaper. See other craft courses. Also teaching china repair under *Leather Worker*, page 54, and *Craft Worker*, page 24).

## Equipment
Students bring their own materials and tools, and their own china to repair.
*Cost* of equipment to start work pro-

fessionally when qualified: Around £260 depending on the brands and quantities used. These vary with the articles being repaired. Equipment includes air brush – about £55, Electric compressor £110, jeweller's drill £60, brushes, paints, glues £30. Air brushes and compressor not strictly necessary as a lot of work can be painted by hand. Try for crafts equipment: 'Winmar' Crafts, 85, Watling Street Road, Fulwood, Preston, Lancs.

## Premises
Working at home is of course much less expensive than having to rent a workshop. One small room could be used as a studio but space is needed for storage of materials; you also need a large worktable and shelves placed high so that chemicals and other materials are kept safely out of the reach of children.

## Write to
Your Local Adult Education Centre, your Local Authority or any local museum for advice. Also, it is worth trying the National Trust or speaking to the warden or curator or guide at any stately home which is in your district. They may know of good classes or private teachers so that you can arrange tuition to suit your own needs.

## Law
You do not need anyone's permission to do this work in your own home. But it is advisable to be extra careful if you have small children. The materials used are attractive to children, so your studio should be kept locked when not in use.

## Advertising
Newsagents' window cards. The glossy specialist magazines concerned with art.

**What you can earn**
Varies considerably; if you can work fast you can obviously earn more.

**Advantages**
The work is interesting and satisfying.

**Disadvantages**
Your earnings will depend to some extent on the value of the articles you are commissioned to mend. A kitchen teapot might take just as long to mend, but you can't charge the same as for a piece of Sevres china.

**Comments**
If I had the talent for it, this is the job I myself would choose – to restore beauty.

## Chiropody   M/F   18–75

Very few costs after initial investment. Very good income. Can be done either at home or by visiting clients.

**Qualifications**
A training course at a School of Chiropody.

**Training**
1. The NHS requires the full 3-year Diploma Course, which leads to State Registration.
2. A shorter course by arrangement with a Chiropody School.
3. Qualification by correspondence course. (This is still allowed, but only for chiropodists who have been practising many years and who are now mostly in their fifties or more. Strictly speaking they may not work for the N.H.S., but many in fact do so because of the serious shortage of chiropodists working in Britain.)

If you are over 18 with five 'O' levels including English and one science subject, you can be admitted to a school. You may be eligible for a grant. There are now eleven Chiropody Schools, two in London, and Birmingham, Edinburgh, Salford, Glasgow, Cardiff, Durham, Huddersfield, Plymouth, Belfast (Northern Ireland) and another is proposed in East Sussex. (See Index for addresses.)

**Equipment**
Chiropodists buy their own bag of tools; perhaps at least £200 worth to start, but they can be purchased secondhand. But when setting up in business at home, the full equipment plus trolley and drill, bought new, can come to £1500 to £4000 for sophisticated equipment; secondhand is cheaper. Get your equipment from 'Footman Chiropody Supplies', 475-479 London Road, Mitcham, Surrey. (Tel: 01-646 2040).

**Premises**
One room for practice, and if possible a small waiting room, in an urban or suburban development. A remote country cottage would hardly attract many clients. Running water in the practice room would be useful but it is not essential.

**Write to**
The Secretary, The Society of Chiropodists, 8 Wimpole Street, London W1M 8BX. The School of Chiropody Chelsea, London SW3 or your local school of chiropody; The London Foot Hospital.

**Law**
Since 1960, the law requires you to be registered with your local authority. Also, it is advisable, for your own protection, to join the Society of Chiropodists (4,200 members). The majority of the membership works privately either in their own home or in rented premises. (Membership fee is £36 p.a.) The Society gives protection by arranging third party insurance for you. It also supplies free a monthly

journal in which 'discreet' advertising is allowed.

### Advertising
In principle this is not allowed. But it is permitted to publish your name and address in the local health clinic, library or similar institution. Also you may keep a notice in your flat or house where it can be seen by passers-by. You may also advertise in the Yellow Pages directory.

### What you can earn
Basic NHS (full-time) about £5,000 (part-time is roughly a proportion of this) with paid holidays, National Insurance etc.
*Private Practice:* Depends on area, between £4.00 and £6.00 per patient per session, average about £5. In 1981 price is expected to reach £6.

### Advantages
Good earnings; no shortage of customers.

### Disadvantages
It is hard work. Not enough time to get out in the fresh air, but, with a private practice, hours can be flexible.

### Comments
Some chiropodists practising today have not had the required training, but are presumed to be qualified by long experience. A new recruit must be qualified through a recognised course.

## *Cleaner and Spring Cleaner*  M/F  18–45

No investment. Low but reliable, steady income. Although you can bring some articles home (such as cutlery, clothing, curtains, small furniture or upholstery) to clean in your own home, this job will necessitate your leaving home for a few hours each day. However, the hours when you *do* work are strictly up to you. Suit yourself.

### Spring cleaning
Wash down all paintwork, brush ceilings, walls, use carpet cleaners on carpets and rugs; vacuum and use upholstery cleaner on upholstered furniture, otherwise use spray or wax polish on all furniture, tables that require it; wash tiled surfaces with scouring powder in kitchen and bathroom; curtain piles or rails to be thoroughly dusted, take down curtains to wash or clean in your own home (depending on material) also loose covers; wash windows and mirrors with chamois leather and crumpled newspaper.

### Qualifications
Health and Vigour. Back pain is sometimes a problem. (See *Useful Contacts*).

### Training
Best done running your own home.

### How to train
Do it. (This is a job where watching TV 'ads' and reading women's magazines is essential to find new, helpful ideas.)

### Equipment
If you work for a bachelor or woman scholar, take your own. Include the following: household gloves, rubber gloves, large pinafore, dungarees, old trousers and shoes; brooms, mops, dusters, old rags, ceiling brushes, feather duster, furniture polish, scouring powder, washing-up liquid, bucket, vacuum cleaner, floor polisher, silver cleaning polish, J-cloths, iron. (Thus equipped, you can charge considerably for your work.)

### Premises
Persuade your employer to let you bring home as much cleaning work as possible. Otherwise work only for your *nearest* neighbours, schools, shops etc. Try never to take work which requires a bus ride or journey.

### Write to
A card in the newsagents' window or a

card with your particulars through doors in your immediate neighbourhood.

**Law**
If you think you are underpaid or overburdened consult C.A.B. to find out your rights.

**Advertising**
See above.

**What you can earn**
£1.20 to £1.50 per hour. *Example:* It can take nine hours a week to clean a large four floor maisonette thoroughly, including washing, bed-linen and tablecloths (shirts for the laundry), collecting all domestic items from local supermarket, making beds.

**Spring cleaner**
Much harder work depending on the size of home. You should charge about £1.50 to £2.00 per hour.

**Advantages**
If you do this work you need never fear unemployment.

**Disadvantages**
You'll need music while you work to get you through.

## Computer Programmer  M/F  18–55

No investment required. Very good income. Can be done at home.

**Qualifications**
You have to be already experienced in computer programming to operate and qualify as a freelance programmer.

ICL (International Computers Limited) who employ many homebound women, make the minimum requirement of 3 years in a particular field of the work, either with their organisation or other recognised computer specialists. They say: 'We only recruit experienced staff, the basis for our attitude is that whilst it's easy to learn new facts working in the home, it is very difficult to acquire new skills'.

This stipulation comes from ICL's Contract Programming Services (CPS), which specialises in organising work at home for programmers, systems analysts and technical authors.

**Training**
You have to have a sound record of performance within the field for which you are recruited. Therefore, a minimum of 3 years full-time in the business is the basic training qualification.

You have to be trained to be familiar with both high and low level programming techniques, in many cases across several machines. Training and employment in computer industries is offered in 'situations vacant' columns regularly in the daily press.

**Equipment**
Whatever equipment is necessary for home-based staff will usually be provided.

**Premises**
A desk at home and a telephone.

**Write to**
The Manager, Contract Programming Services, International Computers Limited, Westfields, West Avenue, Kidsgrove, Stoke-on-Trent, ST7 1TL (Tel: Stoke-on-Trent 29681). (Also see *Useful Contacts* for other firms).

**Law**
No restrictions.

**Advertising**
No restrictions.

**What you can earn**
Equivalent rates of payment to those of full-time site-based staff.

**Advantages**
Even with a large family of small children, you will be able to earn a satisfactory income. It is one of the few jobs helped and encouraged by management for you to do at home.

You should be able to commit yourself to 16 hours a week, also to travel sometimes to attend meetings.

**Disadvantages**
You must be an experienced Computer Programmer. I read all the materials very kindly sent to me by CPS and couldn't understand a word of it.

## Confectioner  M/F  25–48

Some investment is necessary. Good income. Can be done at home.

**Qualifications**
Talent for imaginative cookery.

**Training**
Domestic science course at an Adult Education College. There are various courses at the W.I.'s Denman College. Evening classes locally. Try to spend a weekend at one of the many fascinating 'Craft Courses'. See *Craft Worker* page 24. Also *Useful Contacts*.

Experiment at home with making small animals and shapes out of marzipan and chocolate. These should first be designed and drawn on paper.

**Equipment**
Good oven and a variety of baking tins, shapes and cutters, as well as a plentiful supply of ingredients.

**Premises**
Your own kitchen.

**Write to**
National Federation of Women's Institutes, 39 Eccleston Street, London SW1W 9NT. Don't forget s.a.e. Or contact your local branch.

**Law**
Food hygiene regulations are strict. Ask the H.M.S.O. for copy of regulations S.I. 1970 No. 1172 (see *Useful Contacts* page 121, for address).
    N.B. Home-made Ice-cream and yoghurt should not be sold to the general public. The restrictions are manifold and salmonella (food poisoning) is an added hazard.

**Advertising**
Advertise locally, papers, newsagents' window, parish magazines, etc.

**What you can earn**
Your margin of profit will not be large because of the high cost of ingredients. Mass-produced sweets can be made much more cheaply because of the large quantities involved. Nevertheless, the whole purpose of this job would be to attract a highly specialised market. So success will largely depend on personal recommendation, and professionalism, i.e. maintenance of standards, prices and delivery dates. A joint enterprise with a friend who can make up suitable gift boxes for special occasions, etc, could improve your market. I know some housewives who are now manufacturing specialist chocolates, using their own recipe. The chocolates are packed in small decorated baskets (used afterwards for pot plants) and sold to big stores.

**Advantages**
A good outlet for imagination and talent.

**Disadvantages**
Sustaining a regular market can mean an uneven workload. Sampling the goods too often could ruin your figure!

# Corsetière  M/F  25–55

Very inexpensive to start and very low investment. Modest income but steady and continuing. Can be done at home or by visiting clients.

## Qualifications
You should be female, between the ages of 25 and 55, in good health and not already employed.

## Training
The big corset-making firms interview recruits and then train them locally (near their own homes), usually for two days a week over three weeks, the hours being about 9.30 a.m. until 4.00 p.m. each day. It is a good idea to do additional study by correspondence, by reading or by evening class for example, take a course in health and nursing so that you know the answers when clients ask your advice on basic medical questions.

Spirella Fashion Service in the Home train recruits by giving instruction in fitting, product knowledge and building a business. Spirella say there are many methods of building up your own business and these are taught during training. They charge each woman recruit £20 towards the cost of training but this sum is refunded at the end of the first year if a specific amount of turnover has been produced. Spirella Consultants and most corset companies provide all equipment.

## Premises
Urban or suburban environment is necessary. One small room is sufficient, but it should be well-heated, and look inviting and clean.

## Write to
The Sales Manager, Spirella Fashions Services in the Home, The Spirella Company of Great Britain Limited, Bridge Road, Letchworth, Herts SG6 4ET (Tel: Letchworth 6161).

Also write to your local Health Clinic for advice and consult your local fashion shops.

## Law
There are no restrictions.

## Advertising
If you decide to go freelance, advertising in local papers, women's magazines and health journals; put a card in your newsagents' window.

## What you can earn
Earnings depend on how many hours you can devote initially to building up your business and reputation. Spirella say: 'There is a very high repeat factor as far as the sale of our garments is concerned and, therefore, providing she gives good service to her customers, there is every possibility she will continue to receive orders from the same customers at regular intervals for the rest of her career'.

## Advantages
Steady, not too demanding, work because it can be done by appointment to suit you.

## Disadvantages
Don't take up this work unless you like women. As with Beauty Counselling (see page 8) you need to be interested and sympathetic in manner.

# Craft Worker  M/F  16–70

Small to medium investment. Medium or fair income. Can be done at home.

## Qualifications
Knowledge, ability or a wish to learn any craft, such as: Bobbin lace-making, crochet (contemporary and fashion), canvas embroidery and other canvas work, embroidery with fabrics, simple toy-making, tie-dye/batik, cane, basketry, knitting finishes, glove-making, knotting and netting, linen

embroidery, patchwork, picture-framing, rag rug-making, rushwork.

Also some of the newer more complicated crafts such as candle-making, enamelling, glass engraving, whittling, hand-spinning, weaving (see *Useful Contacts*). (Also quilting, which is quite different work from patchwork quilting, see page 67.)

## Training
Evening Classes, adult education institutes or any County College of Further Education. Also tuition given by the National Federation of Women's Institutes. Denman College – write sending a s.a.e. for their 1980 brochure showing the many courses in crafts. (Denman College courses for 1981 range from £22.10 for a weekend to £45.40 for the Monday-Friday course (roughly £11.35 per day including accommodation) (See *Useful Contacts*). Or you can take a weekend course at West Dean College, Chichester, West Sussex, the cost of which includes food and accommodation is £39.50. Write for Prospectus. For other courses, see *Leather Worker*, page 54.

## Equipment
For those who are not members of the Women's Institute, there are a number of firms supplying all the materials needed for craftwork. One of them is Fred Aldous Limited, The Handicraft Centre, P.O. Box No. 135, 37 Lever Street, Manchester M60 1UX (Tel: 061-236 2477). They provide a full price list and illustrated catalogue for 15p part-postage. They do *not* buy any of your work. You have to find your own customers.

## Premises
Your own workroom at home, with cupboards for tools and equipment.

## Write to
First to the Administrative Secretary, Crafts Department of the W.I. You can become a member for very little money and benefit by their advice and training as well as help in selling your stuff. You must send a large s.a.e. Also COSIRA (the Government sponsored Council for Small Industries in Rural Areas, 141, Castle Street, Salisbury, Wilts SP1 3TP. COSIRA organisers cover every county in England (see *Useful Contacts* for COSIRA addresses in Scotland and Wales.)

If you are self-employed or employ up to 20 skilled people in a rural area or country town, they may give you a loan for your workshop or equipment or as working capital. Initial advice is free; after that they will tell you the standard rate of charge.

For details of other craft courses, try the Booking Secretary, Dillington House, Ilminster, Somerset TA19 9DT. A residential short course booklet is available from the National Institute of Adult Education 19b De Monfort Street, Leicester LE1 7GE. Try one-day courses or Saturday courses to learn enamelling at The Old Mill, Mannerch, Nr. Mold Co. Clwyd, Wales or at The Enamel Shop, 21 Macklin Street, London WC2. (Tel: 01-242 7053). Also for candle-making and glass engraving. For information on Courses and Crafts, the Design Council at 28 Haymarket, London SW1 (Tel: 01-839 8000) publish a booklet entitled *Design Courses in Britain*, price £1.25 (add 20p if you order by post).

Included are painters, potters, design bookbinders, design and research for gold, silver and jewellery industries, glass and handworkers, engravers, scribes and illuminators, weavers, spinners and dyers and so on. . . .

## Law
There are no restrictions on craftwork at home.

## Advertising
You can advertise locally in papers, rural magazines, parish magazines, at local fetes and in shop windows.

**What you can earn**
You must obviously cover your actual cost of materials and any general expenses, but how you cost your time out is a moot point. If it were costed at office rates, most crafts would not sell. I really think all one can advise is that people wander all around the various craft galleries and see the general pricing of items, although crafts in many galleries are over-priced and of a poor standard. If anyone is very keen on crafts and is not a W.I. member it is an ideal thing to join.

**Advantages**
Creative and therefore satisfying work. There are fascinating week-end residential courses in all crafts and suddenly it is very much the 'in' thing to learn enamelling, glass engraving, quilting, weaving, spinning, cookery arts etc. etc. (See *Useful Contacts* for all of these.)

**Disadvantages**
May not be a big earner at first but it could become one.

## Dance teacher    M/F    15–50

*(or Children's Dance School)*

Small investment, if you have your own piano or other musical instrument or a good record player. Good return for only a few hours of work per week. Can be done at home.

**Qualifications**
A talent for music and some experience of dancing-lessons, either at school or at a private dancing-class. Best of all is experience of ballet classes or of a good local keep-fit class routine. Some teaching experience is helpful, especially gymnastics, physical culture, swimming or sport. You don't have to be Olga Korbut but it helps if you take a special interest in watching that kind of gymnastic display on television. Some experience of children.

**Training**
Take a short course in ballet or any specialist dancing, including ballroom dancing (of the kind popular on TV), and/or study books on the art of ballet. Attend your local disco regularly. Try Dance Teachers Association International, 76 Bennett Road, Brighton (Tel: Brighton (0273) 685652) and get *Dance Teacher* monthly magazine.

**Equipment**
This work is only suitable for a person living not too far from a school or schools, who has a large empty room at home with a suitable floor (or one which can be treated to make it suitable for dancing). A room with central heating if possible, and preferably in an older type of house, with a high ceiling, and almost no furniture in it except a piano.

**Premises**
The whole point of doing this kind of job is to use your own home, with its empty room or heated garden outside buildings etc. Most British pre-war towns and villages had private dancing schools of this kind, usually run by 'daughters of the house' who were not allowed to leave home to have a more commercial career. It became a 'craze' that developed between the Wars, when mothers thought it important for their sub-teenage children to try and learn the social graces, which then included doing some sort of 'Charleston', 'Tango' and 'Black Bottom'. The reasoning was that girls who couldn't master these complicated steps had little hope of marriage! The fashion for young teenage dancing-lessons has returned more recently. At Edenbridge in Kent, for instance, schoolchildren attend ballet classes after school. There are sound reasons why this is a good idea, for, say, a Mother with a young

family. It provides a safe, fascinating, warmly social atmosphere for after-school hours, and does it locally in districts where youngsters can safely walk home in the dark or bad weather.

The idea is to provide basically Junior instruction but to have, say, one evening a week, dancing lessons for adults and children.

### Write to

Because this work involves children, you must write to your Local Authority first to tell them of your plan. Having informed them, just go ahead. Then write to the Principal of all your local schools, and if possible show them that you have had previous experience of, say, infant teaching, Montessori work, sport training, social work and that you have at some time attended a dancing class or physical culture unit.

### Law

Why not call in at your Town Hall and have a chat with someone in the Education Department . . . just to cover yourself. You might find you have to pay an additional insurance premium against Fire, Loss of Property, Damage or Accident. Although any work with children must be treated with the utmost serious-ness, (i.e. you must show you are a responsible person). Do not be fright-ened off by interfering busybodies.

### Advertising

Best kind of 'ad' for this work is the recommendation of friends, especially schoolfriends, but try the card-through-the-door approach or print some leaflets of the kind I have seen in some towns and villages, where Barn Dances are of course a regular form of entertainment.

### What you can earn

It depends on your qualifications. If you are a qualified Dance Instructor, you will charge accordingly. If you decide to provide some refreshments, teas, coffees, ices, sandwiches etc. (useful for schoolchildren who may have had scratch lunches) then you must cover expenses and make a profit. Remember you will get tax relief, not only on lighting, heating, rent and rates, but also on your hair-do, clothes, make-up etc., because an attractive appearance is necessary for your business.

### Advantages

If you can attract local teenagers to your place and away from the com-mercial discos in the High Street, the whole town will adore you!

### Disadvantages

You will have to diet, keep slim and fit as this is your best 'ad' for business.

---

## Doll restorer    F    14–65

### (and Repairer)

Investment could be small or large. If large, income could be very high. Recently, this business has snowballed from being a fascinating hobby yield-ing a small income to Very Big Busi-ness, including export trade, partly perhaps thanks to publicity on TV.

### Qualifications

Needlework skills, some knowledge of costume fashions and the history of fashion.

### Training

Best training is love of dolls and ex-perience in handling them, from childhood onwards. Example: Mrs Daphne Fraser who has her own collection of over 50 valuable, historic dolls, began at the age of three, 'when I mended my own dolls'. Even felt or rag dolls have value if they are old enough, but today's market is mainly for the bisque (china) dolls. Says Mrs Fraser: 'Germany seems to have cornered the market in valuable, antique dolls, each worth some thousands of pounds, but

France is also an eager market for buying and selling them. The French taste is for Jumeau dolls, valued at between £60 and over £1,000.

## How to train
Evening classes or craft course, similar to china repair (see page 19). Some of the short weekend courses mentioned in *Leather Worker* (page 54) and *Craft Worker* (page 24) also teach this kind of china repair. (Many rag dolls have unglazed china heads.) Also visit Doll Museums (see *Useful Contacts*) in Edinburgh and Tunbridge Wells. You can get good experience from attending antique sales (Sotheby's, Christie's or on Country estates.) Learn to recognise genuine antique dolls by looking for the manufacturer's mark, which has been fired into the pins to make an impression and reveals the date when made. Read books on the history of doll making. A good one is Audrey Johnson's *How to Repair and Dress old Dolls*, published by G. Bell and Sons Ltd., London. Also visit Madam Tussaud's in London and Brighton. (Another Scots doll expert, Mrs Jan Wightman of Fife, learned by studying old photograph albums of Victorian and Edwardian costumes and children's annuals like *Our Darlings*, *Jolly Book*, *Wonder Book* and so on.)

## Equipment
Look in your attic for teddy bears, rag dolls, any favourite doll of your grandmother's. Use a button hook to pull elastic through bodices, spoon handles to smooth cracked wax faces. You also need a sewing machine, sewing/crochet equipment and all your china repair equipment, glue etc.

## Premises
A safe, uncluttered room to yourself with cupboard for tools, books etc. Work at home of course.

## Write to
Mrs Daphne Fraser, Glenbarry, Victoria Road, Lenzie, Near Glasgow. (Tel: 041-776 1281). Also to the craft centres (see *Useful Contacts* page 121).

## Law
No restrictions.

## Advertising
Exhibit your work at sales etc.

## What you can earn
Study the methods of antique dealers at sales and auctions. If you are skilled enough to restore a genuine antique doll, ask any price you like between £100 and £1,000 or more.

## Advantages
It's fun!

## Disadvantages
Like china repair work it's slow and painstaking work, you need good eyesight and nimble fingers.

---

# *Dressmaker* M/F 18–70

---

Some investment. Good or very good income. Can be done at home.

## Qualifications
A natural aptitude for sewing and making clothes. Ability to use a sewing-machine.

## Training
One way to obtain a qualification is to attend a technical college for about 200 hours and be entered as a candidate for, possibly, a City & Guilds examination; or GCE 'O' and 'A' level examinations. However, such a qualification would usually be necessary only for teaching purposes.

Another way is to take the correspondence courses provided by the International Correspondence School, Intertext House, Stewarts Road, London SW8 4UJ (Tel: 01-622 9911).

One course is planned to train you to be able to make clothes for adults and children quickly and expertly.

There is also a course in pattern cutting and designing, which is a professional course and not really suitable for the absolute beginner. But courses are not cheap at £70 upwards. So try your Local Authority evening classes for pattern-making, etc.

The Institute awards a certificate on successful completion of a course – useful to have on display.

### Equipment
You will need a dummy bust (about £25 new), adjustable to all measurements; also scissors, shears, needle and thread, iron and ironing board and some basic patterns. A new sewing machine can cost over £100 with attachments for button-holes and fancy stitching. But secondhand is adequate, and costs £25 or less if you search jumble sales (see *Junk Restorer* page 50).

### Premises
A room at home, with suitable electric points, where you can leave things out.

### Write to
Your Local Adult Education Centre, for advice on classes.

### Law
There are no restrictions on dress-making at home.

### Advertising
Cards in newsagents' windows; your personal card through local letter-boxes. Personal recommendation is the best method.

### What you can earn
Fix your prices by asking around the shops, friends, contacts. You may feel uncomfortable asking the full rate for the job when doing work for friends, and therefore you must make it clear that you are in business and working for a living. Do this before accepting an order from any friend.

### Advantages
The job fits in most conveniently with a normal household; even the starting and stopping that goes with the care of young children. It is creative and satisfying.

### Disadvantages
Talented home-dressmakers are sometimes exploited by friends, relations and even husbands!

---

# Driving instructor   M/F   20–50

---

You need your own car. Low investment. High income. Can be done from home or by visiting pupils.

### Qualifications
Your name must be in the Register of Approved Driving Instructors; or you must hold a trainee's licence issued by the Registrar (see below).

### Training
You have to be able to pass the examination for entry to the Register. It consists of a written and practical part. Details of the examination and how to pass it are given in a booklet issued by the Department of Transport, 2 Marsham Street, London SW1 (Tel: 01-212 3434 for general enquiries.)

While training for practical experience, you must hold a trainee's licence to give driving instruction. Until registered, you must obtain supervision by a registered instructor when working from your own home or from a school.

Both the written and practical parts of the examination test ability to instruct as well as ability to drive. (The Register of Approved Driving Instructors warned me that it is not enough to be a good driver.) The pass rate in the examination is about 60%.

### Equipment
Suitable saloon motor car or estate car in sound condition. Until you are registered it must be free from advertisements or signs which might cause other road users to believe that it is being used for driving instruction. It should have non-automatic transmission system, right-hand steering, a readily adjustable driving seat and seat for a forward facing front passenger. Two L-Plates should be carried for attachment to the vehicle when required.

### Premises
Registered instructors can work from home, so of course a telephone and garage are sufficient.

### Write to
The Registrar of Approved Driving Instructors (as above) at the Department of Transport (Tel: 01-212 3434) or write to any of the Department's Traffic Area Offices. These are the offices to which applications for driving tests are sent.

### Law
The car must be insured for the examiner's liability for all third-party and damage risks and for his liability to any passenger, including any official passenger.

Your official title is 'Department of Transport Approved Driving Instructor' and you get a licence to give professional instruction only from the address specified in the licence (see Form ADI 14 issued by the Department of Transport). The name of the applicant is entered in the Register when qualified and you receive an official Certificate of Registration incorporating your name, photograph and official title; this certificate is suitable for exhibiting in the car you use for tuition.

*Fees:* The fee for admission to the written part of the Register Examination is (at present) £15.00. Successful candidates are required to pay a further fee of £35 before taking the practical part. If you fail, you can try again at the same cost as before.

### Advertising
When registered, you are allowed to advertise in your local evening paper, newsagent etc. However, if you want to display a notice in your windows, consult C.A.B. or the Council first.

### What you can earn
Many schools now charge between £6 and £8 per hour, but as low as £3.50 if you can book 20 lessons in advance. You can fix your own charges, so the earnings capabilities are excellent.

### Advantages
You can work whatever hours suit you or your clients. That is, weekends, holidays, early and late and any times when pupils are free from work and when you can safely leave the children with someone at home.

### Disadvantages
I once had a handsome blond instructor who told me that most of his women pupils tried to make love to him! There is also a lot of wear and tear on your vehicle.

---

## English Teacher   M/F   25–35

*(for Foreigners and Immigrants)*

No investment, modest income from teaching immigrants; high income from teaching foreign business people. Can be done at home.

### Qualifications
Thorough knowledge of English.

### Training
This work is suitable for, say, a house-

wife who has a couple of hours each day to be alone and free. Specially suitable for the middle-aged man or woman but also for a housewife whose children are at school.

**How to train**
If you have brought up children and helped them with reading and spelling, this is probably sufficient.

**Equipment**
A quiet room at home, table, books, pencils, possibly a radio and/or tapes.

**Premises**
(As above.) This job is done almost always at home, but in the case of Asian girls under about 17 you may be asked to visit their home – unless you can persuade their parents that your home is a safe place!

**Write to**
Your Local Authority or to any Social Club. Also try your local hospital, where foreign nursing staff are given time off for English tuition. If you live in a more rural area you could start your own English class for au-pair girls to save their having to go into town. Also write to local factories employing foreign working people.

**Law**
No restrictions unless young children are concerned. Ask Citizens Advice Bureau for advice.

**Advertising**
The usual newsagents' card.

**What you can earn**
It is really up to your conscience, but for Asian immigrants, the Local Authority decide what they will pay. If you are a good teacher/communicator, I suggest £2 per hour for each pupil is not too high; or you could take several pupils together.

For Europeans (French, German, Italian, Spanish or Portuguese) some factories in the Home Counties are paying more than £10 an hour to English teachers with no special teaching qualifications. You do not have to speak any foreign language . . . only good *English*!

**Advantages**
Interesting work you can do at home.

**Disadvantages**
You might end up speaking better French or Hindu!

---

## *Envelope addresser*   M/F   17–70

---

No investment. Very small income. Can be done at home.

**Qualifications**
Ability to write clearly and/or an ability to type accurately and fast.

**Training**
None required.

**Write to**
Firms requiring envelope-addressers will be found in the Yellow Pages directories.
*For advice try:* This firm handle mass distribution 'Distribution and Media Sales (UK) Ltd, Bridge Road Industrial Estate, Haywards Heath, Sussex (Tel: Haywards Heath (0444) 52255/57876), speak to Richard Fry or Ian Cameron.

**What you can earn**
Rates are varied but are admitted to be low for all the effort.
*Warning:* This is one of the jobs under the special attention of the hundreds of C.A.B.'s (Citizens Advice Bureaux) throughout the country. C.A.B. Offices welcome information about 'bad' employers who exploit workers

with bad pay but such information is *always* treated in the strictest confidence for obvious reasons.

### Advantages
It is the kind of work you can do even if you've got a lot of other things on your mind at the time.

### Disadvantages
It is extremely boring so perhaps this job could be alternated with something else.

## Flower arranger   M/F   18–20

### (and Florist)

Some reasonable, not high investment needed. Modest income. Can be done at home or from home but transport is essential.

Flower arranging; freelance by helping your local florist for special jobs such as weddings and local parties etc. You can also earn modest sums by lecturing, demonstrating and giving local lessons on flower arrangement, concentrating on Ikebana or other speciality designs. Floristry: start by buying plants and seeds cheaply and potting in your own hand-painted pots which can then be exhibited on someone's local market stall or your own stall outside your garden gate.

### Qualifications and training
A knowledge of the art of flower-arranging, and some knowledge of floristry. There are lots of books on the various methods of flower arranging.

Take private lessons (e.g. from a local evening class teacher) or become a qualified florist by courses of study at the College of Horticulture, Wisbech, Cambridgeshire. You can also qualify by day-release training or study at National Federation of Women's Institutes (N.F.W.I.'s), Denman College, Marcham, Abingdon, Oxon.

Ask for advice at your local flower nursery, or at a local college of horticulture, or at the Constance Spry School.

Work an apprenticeship at your local flower shop, or do part time Sunday work at a local flower nursery.

### Premises and equipment
To do floristry on any scale you need a garden and a greenhouse (perhaps a balcony would do).

However, for flower arranging you need only space in a cool shed to store cut flowers bought from your local market overnight.

Many of our stately homes make additional money by selling off their plants and garden produce at the gate at low prices and they are worth a visit sometimes for this reason alone.

### Write to
Your local flower club. This is affiliated to the N.A.F.A.S. (The National Association of Flower Arrangement Societies) 21a Denbigh Street, London SW1. The Constance Spry School, 74 Marylebone Lane, London W1 (Tel: 01-499 7201) (recognised by the Department of Education and Science); Mrs Violet Jenkins S.F. Dip., Honorary Secretary, College of Horticulture, Newcommon Bridge, Wisbech, Cambridgeshire PE13 2SJ (Tel: Wisbech 2561, ext. 246/7).

(There is a waiting list for courses at both the Constance Spry School and at the College of Horticulture. So if you are keen on high qualifications write for advice to the Society of Floristry, 6 Arnold Lane. Whittlesey, Cambs, PE7 1QD. And ask for the two year course leading to a City & Guilds Certificate. You can also train to be a non-vocational decorator for flower clubs'.)

### Law
No restrictions.

**Advertising**
Do this locally with a card in newsagents' window.

**What you can earn**
It's a good idea to specialise in weddings, parties where earnings are high.

**Advantages**
Statistics show that after motoring, gardening is Britain's most-loved pastime, hobby and art.

**Disadvantages**
A business dealing in so perishable a stock must run a great risk. You've got to be a bit of a gambler.

---

## Foster parent  M/F  Over 35

---

No investment needed. Regular income. Must be done at home.

**Qualifications**
A stable home of your own (husband and own children not essential, as they often used to be in former years).

The kind of home preferred is neither too luxurious nor too tidy, but cosy, lived-in. Men and women over 35 are preferred, but this is not a hard and fast rule. Working wives are liked, because this is nowadays normal for mothers and it is believed beneficial for foster-children to experience the same difficulties that other children of working mothers have. Foster-parents are wanted for short-term (up to three months), and long-term (up to age 18).

**Training**
There are a number of training schemes for foster parents; some organised by Local Authorities but a good training is provided by the National Foster Care Association which started in May 1974. There are over 50 N.F.C.A. Groups in Britain and over 5,000 members.

**How to train**
The training consists of information, help and support given to new foster-parents by those already experienced. They visit where possible, write, telephone and give advice on the spot to new foster-parents faced with problems.

**Equipment**
It is useful if you have already got a bed, bedding and/or spare room or rooms for your new foster-child or children, but if not, you will get financial help and full payment for everything you have to buy for the child e.g. new clothes, bedding, even birthday and Christmas presents and pocket money (Every Local Authority and religious organisation has its own methods and rules, so it is important to find out in advance what to expect. For example, some Councils will pay in advance for the child's extra needs in clothes etc: others may expect you to lay out the money first and you will be paid in arrears with your next month's fees.)

**Premises**
Some Local Authorities will help you to get a mortgage to buy a house if you accept a certain number of foster-children. However, this does NOT apply to all Councils. You would be more likely to get such help if you already had fostered children for a number of years.

**Write to**
National Foster Care Association, Francis House, Francis Street, London SW1 (Tel: 01-828 6266 (Mrs Manchego.))

The Church of England Children's Society, Old Town Hall, Kennington

Road, London SE11 4QD (Tel: 01-735 2441).

Children's Departments at your local Council Offices. (Some Local Authorities have various new schemes to recruit more foster-parents, they include Birmingham, Croydon, Berkshire, Dunbartonshire, Northamptonshire, Kent and Reading Councils. Some of these schemes are experimental).

## Law

New laws and regulations concerning both fostering and adoption came into force in the United Kingdom with the new Children's Bill which became law in January 1976.

You should get a copy of all the new laws from H.M.S.O. Holborn, London. (See *Useful Contacts*).

### Advertising

In recent years newspapers, magazines, radio and television have sometimes advertised for foster-parents. (Kent County Council was one of the first to permit publicity in local papers in 1974 with photographs of children etc.) and children have appeared on television.

It is illegal to advertise yourself as a foster-parent (although this still happens but whenever possible social workers try to stop it). Unregistered child-minders or 'foster-parents' can be prosecuted.

### What you can earn

Do remember before you even start to consider this work that this is not a profit-motivated occupation; however, fees payable to foster-parents vary according to the Local Authority. The N.F.C.A. warn that not all Local Authorities can afford to pay high rates for fostering, especially after Government cuts. Payment in some poorer rural areas may still be low.

Some of the highest rates are paid by the G.L.C. for the London area and another of the more generous Authorities (after the G.L.C.) is Croydon

Council. As a guide, here are the 1980 fostering rates quoted by the Church of England Children's Society: Up to age 4 £15.26 per week, 5–7 £17.85; 8–10 £19.53; 11–12 £21.21; 13–15 £22.89; 16–18 £27.16. Extra payments for birthdays and Christmas.

As the cost of keeping a child in a Residential Home is over £100 per week it is obvious that Local Authorities are anxious to recruit more foster-parents as it saves them a great deal of money, quite apart from the fact that a long stay in residential care in a children's home is considered bad for the child. Children become withdrawn owing to lack of personal, continuing attention by the same person or persons. (See *Useful Contacts* for addresses of the Society's many Regional Offices.)

### Advantages

If you like children and enjoy seeing them grow happily, this can be a most rewarding job. (I investigated this side of fostering in some detail in 1970 when I wrote a book called *Only Uncle* about a Surrey bachelor who fostered 12 small children for 10 years. The hero of this book later became the centre of a fictionalised BBC television series with Ian Carmichael playing the role of Bachelor Father.)

### Disadvantages

There are three main ones. First you must be willing to allow visits (usually once a month) from a social worker who will want to interview the child alone without your listening in. This is, however, a sensible precaution and usually helps the foster-parent who can put any of her own problems during this monthly 'inspection'.

You may also have to receive one or both of the natural parents to give them tea or a meal (if they've come a long journey) and be friendly. This might perhaps be a visiting mother who has been sentenced for battering her baby and later hopes to have the child returned to her.

Also a very large number of children who need fostering may come to you with personality problems, which may take the form of delinquency, lying, stealing, wetting the bed and so on.

However, you will get full support from some marvellous and remarkable men and women who run the above-mentioned National Foster Care Association and will come rushing to your aid if you telephone a local member for advice. Lastly, you can grow to love a child as your own in a very short time and legally it can be removed from your care at short notice for a variety of reasons – its natural parents being in a position to take it back is one of the most frequent. (However, the new Children's Bill devised by Dr David Owen which became law in 1976 does nowadays supply some safeguards against your having your heart broken too ruthlessly, e.g. if Lawyers can prove that it is in the best interests of the child to stay with you.)

---

## French Polisher   M/F   30–60

---

No investment, big income when qualified. Can be done at home.

### Qualifications
Training and experience. You must be a careful, conscientious person because you are handling inflammable materials. Good eyesight.

### Training
Contact your Local Adult Education Institute.

### How to train
Best way is apprenticeship to a Furniture Dealer or Furniture Supplier. Also study one of many books on the art of French Polishing, such as *The Finishing and Refining of Wood* by Frederick Oughton, published by Constable (ask at your library). Also ask 'Brass Tacks' Furniture Restoration Supervisors Mr Huw Roberts or John Pratt (Tel: 01-249 9461).

### Equipment and Premises
Although this is work you can do at home, it is dangerous because you will be surrounded by bottles or cans of inflammable spirit, like Methylated spirits, White spirits, and the French Polish itself (which stains your hands brown for a few days). I have watched several housewives who do this work in their own garages (cars have to stand in the front garden). You need a strong light in the winter; possibly a convector heater. *Never* smoke or allow any naked flame near you.

Your work involves sandpapering wooden furniture, e.g. chairs of beech or mahogany. You need plenty of space so that you can leave work overnight and also leave one article to dry while you start on another, e.g. you might have 6 or 8 chairs delivered to your garage for you to spend the whole week french-polishing. Best premises would be a safe, warm, dry shed at the bottom of your garden, with electricity. Keep children *OUT*.

### Write to
Your local upholstery and furniture dealers, also antique dealers. It is also advisable, for your own sake, to contact your local Fire Service, let them visit and advise you on all safety measures.

### Law
You are not breaking the law, but for your own safety and comfort take advice, inform your insurance people, and if your garage is exposed, put up a notice of warning about smoking, naked flames etc.

### Advertising
Newsagents' card, furniture dealers, magazines.

**What you can earn**
It depends on the value of the chairs. I am told about from £6 per chair to £16.

**Advantages**
You learn about the history of furniture, which is a good way to learn history.

**Disadvantages**
I have women friends who do this work at home and they worry about their stained hands. However, they usually do a three day week, so for four days they have clean, white hands.

## Genealogist   M/F   18–80

No investment necessary. *Warning:* Owing to the recent increase in the cost of obtaining certificates (Birth, marriage, death) this is not as lucrative as it once was.

Can be done at home. (Except for outside research work.)

**Qualifications**
Journalist and secretarial experience useful. Typing and note taking should be learned. You must have a thorough knowledge of how to use a library, an intense interest in people; a good, broad education but no specialist knowledge is strictly necessary. Good eyesight.

**Training**
Read as much history as possible. Gain knowledge of how church and parish records are kept.

**How to train**
Get yourself a thorough knowledge of British History. Read all about our stately homes and the people who live in them and visit as many as possible. Read about Scots, Welsh and Irish history also. Study the W.I. course 'Heraldry and Family Records' at Denman College (see *Useful Contacts*).

**Equipment**
A good magnifying glass, typewriter, telephone and as many directories such as *Who's Who* etc. as possible.

Subscriptions to Commonwealth or international newspapers. You will have to spend many hours in libraries, in the British Museum, in researching parish records in ancient churches, visiting the Public Records Office and many local or national museums. But your work of writing and assembling your notes can all be done at home, so that it is up to you just how much time you have to be away from home, researching for clients who want to trace their ancestors centuries back.

**Write to**
The Secretary, The Society of Genealogists, 37 Harrington Gardens, London SW7 4JX (Tel: 01-373 7054) and ask for an application form to join this organisation.

Entrance to all members is £5 the annual subscription for town members (i.e. residing within a radius of 25 miles of Trafalgar Square) is £15 and for Country and Overseas Members £10 not liable for VAT. (If you do not know a Member who can propose and second you, the Executive Committee will be willing to accept a letter of recommendation from a Minister of Religion, Justice of the Peace, Bank Manager or similar responsible person to whom you are known.) Find out what the Society can offer by making a day visit, which costs £4, they have an extensive library and transcripts of some parish registers.

**Law**
Remember that material researched in the archives and on behalf of your clients may be confidential and you may have to get permission from persons concerned for using it publicly, otherwise you are in danger

of possibly infringing clients' own copyright. Protect yourself against all these and other risks by becoming a member of the Society of Genealogists as above.

### Advertising
You are allowed to advertise for clients in papers and journals as well as placing such advertisements in foreign papers abroad, e.g. Australia, America, South Africa and so on, where British descendants who wish to trace their lineage abound.

### What you can earn
You will have to charge according to your expenses, the time spent in travelling, researching; if it can be evaluated, according to the means of your clients. Ask for a substantial deposit according to the size of the job involved. Fees can be related to results the same way as done by *Marriage Bureau* (see page 56).

### Advantages
Fascinating work.

### Disadvantages
Nowadays, alas, the person doing this job really needs a small pension to make a decent living, owing to the higher costs mentioned above. Be on your guard against your own family relations who may want you to research their origins free of charge. This job now has the same risk as Dressmaking and Doctoring. Harden your heart and insist on payment.

---

## *Gardener*  M/F  16–60

### *(Also Jobbing Gardener, Allotment holder)*

No investment to start. Can be done at home, or in your nearest allotment, or in your neighbours' gardens for the share-a-garden scheme. Good, steady, income. Highest income for jobbing gardener work.

### Qualifications
Good health. Best to start about 16.

### Training
Go to your nearest market garden, nursery or large country estate; ask if they'll take you on and teach you. Trainees are usually paid for their work. Or . . . you could take a Horticulture degree at, say, Reading University. Women students (only) go to Studley College in Worcestershire to specialise in gardening, or join the W.I. (See *Useful Contacts*) and study vegetable and herb gardening etc.

### How to train
Best method is to plunge in and *DO* it, while at the same time studying a good, simple gardening book. Daniel Lloyd, 'Heather Lea', 4 Hillcrest Avenue, Chertsey, Surrey specialises in selling secondhand gardening books. Also try studying *The Culture of Vegetables and Flowers* by Sutton & Sons (seed manufacturers), and read *Plain Vegetable Growing* by G. E. Whitehead, published by Blackie. Mr Whitehead trained the man who became head gardener at Buckingham Palace who in turn trained my friend Josephine Ferguson of East Meon, Hants. (Another way to train is as Josephine's cousin did it. She just went along to the Greenhouse in Hyde Park and asked if she could work there; she ended up working for two years at Kensington Palace for Princess Margaret.)

There is also a TOPS course i.e. Government Training course in landscape gardening; information can be got from your local Exchange or Job Centre.

### Equipment
Spade, Fork (a lady's border fork is lighter) hoe and rake. Secateurs for

pruning roses and shrubs. All are expensive now an average of £8 each at Woolworths, but well-known makes cost even more in ironmongers and garden centres. Buy secondhand from junk shops. Auction sales sometimes sell 'a bundle of garden tools' for a fiver. If you work as a Jobbing Gardener tools are provided, by your employer.

Try to hire a nearby allotment and sell your produce. Ask your Local Authority. It is a rule that you *must* work there at least one half-day a week. Ask if you can join the 'Share-a-garden' scheme at your local Town Hall. Young people are sometimes needed, mainly by elderly folk, to cultivate their gardens in exchange for a share in the produce. *Women* gardeners are preferred. You can make a good profit from your own garden if you have several members in your family willing to work unpaid. But you really need to spend on a glass or polythene greenhouse to bring on tomatoes and cucumbers etc.

**Premises**
Use (a) your own garden (b) your allotment (c) your greenhouse and (d) your kitchen window-sill. The allotment is the most productive, but many large towns have a waiting-list and you have to wait until someone gets thrown off their plot for neglecting it! It is most profitable simply to grow bedding plants. You need a large, warm kitchen with broad window-sills. Try and grow one lot for sale in Spring and another lot for Autumn planting. Lettuce plants, cabbage plants and boxes of flower seeds are most profitable.

**Write to**
Your Local Authority and ask permission to use your garden produce for sale; also get from them the address of your nearest allotments and the name of the Secretary of their 'Share-a-garden' Scheme.

**Law**
You do not need permission to use your own garden to sell fruit and veg to the public, unless you suddenly decide to plough up the whole garden for this purpose, which means Change-of-Use (see Chapter 3 *Organising*), when you should tell your District Council as it might affect your rates. Individual Local Councils have differing attitudes as regards this law. Many turn a blind eye to your Change-of-Use if your plot is small.

**Advertising**
All my neighbours do it by placing several buckets outside their gates containing fruit, veg and flowers, also a money box for the money and a chalked notice of the price per lb., or per bunch. Some put a small weighing machine for tomatoes. Cost to advertise in say, greengrocers, or other shop-window is usually 5p per week or 5p per word in the local paper.

**What you can earn**
Jobbing Gardeners (men) now charge £4 per hour; some women charge only £1.30. A friend of mine who charges £2 per hour, does an 8-hour day, netting her £16 per day. Her newsagents' window card says: 'Lady Gardener for your border, tidying, weeding, grass-cutting, hedge-trimming, hours by arrangement, phone . . .'.
*Profit* on seeds; a packet of seeds cost from 29p to 40p. Charge 20p to 30p per plant, which means a good profit!

**Advantages**
Work when you feel like it; otherwise don't!

**Disadvantages**
Rain and snow. Also rabbits, deer, birds, slugs may devour your profit.

Medium to high investment (you could spend up to £45 for a kid). Medium to good income. Can be done at home.

## Qualifications

An interest and affection for animals. Knowledge of goats. Be ready and able to milk the goats twice every day.

## Training

Visit a Member of the British Goat Society. Their Headquarters is at Rougham, Bury St Edmunds, Suffolk, but if you telephone them at Beyton (0351) 03597 you will get an address or telephone number of a member living near to you.

## How to train

Study *An Introduction to the Goat* published by the British Goat Society of the above address. For example, 'goats require milking twice a day, seven days a week, and unless you accept this obligation you cannot expect to get the best from your animal . . . Yields vary from two pints a day to fourteen pints a day.'

A wide variety of literature is obtainable from this Society and you are advised to study this before purchasing, also try and visit a goat show and arrange to visit an established breeder in your area.

## Equipment and Premises

Housing is necessary as goats prefer dry conditions and will not thrive when cold and wet.

Main requirements are protection from wind and rain with plenty of light and freedom from draughts; a good bed of straw should also be provided, and a solid floor which can be washed out.

The goat is an adaptable animal and can live free range, with access to shrubby undergrowth, and will eat brambles, nettles, thistles – as well as grass, of course. But it will also do quite well with just a yard to exercise in, with supervised walks (on the end of a chain), but supplementary feed will be necessary. Clean drinking water should be available at all times.

For a good milk yield, feed of concentrates should be given twice a day with roughage – depending on what the animal can easily forage for itself. Hay, kale, mangolds, sugar beet pulp, surplus vegetables will all make adequate roughage.

Cost of feeding depends on how much you can provide from your garden or other sources and how much you need to buy.

## Write to

The British Goat Society at the above address. Membership includes a monthly journal, year book and herd book, in addition to the facilities for registration and transfer of stock. There are various grades of membership. B.G.S. membership is £8 per year and entitles you to a year book, a hand book and 12 monthly journals.

## Law

This varies from one Local Authority to another. Consult your Local Health Officers about your Council's particular rules for sterilising milk bottles, and/or for printing your name on bottles or cartons.

## Advertising

This is often not necessary because demands exceeds supply. Goat milk, cheese and yoghurt is especially good for invalids and infants and is used to treat infantile eczema, asthma and other digestive disorders. Your local health food shop is likely to take all the milk you can supply.

## What you can earn

Earnings can be high but against that must be set the high cost of feeding;

much depends on whether you raise them intensively or extensively.

**Advantages**
The high yield of milk, providing a surplus to make cheese, cream and yoghurt.

**Disadvantages**
The constant attention means you can't have a day off very often – if ever! Goats get lonely and to keep just one nanny would not be a good idea. The bleating of one goat could upset the neighbours.

## *Hairdresser  M/F   21–60*

Fairly substantial investment. Excellent income. Can be done at home or on visits to local clients.

**Qualifications**
You must be qualified. Do not attempt this work without proper training. The National Federation of Hairdressers tell me that they do not approve of unqualified or freelance hairdressers. They are very fussy about keeping up professional standards and they are quite right in that respect! Therefore, it is up to you to attend as many classes and study courses as possible so that your work is truly professional.

**Training**
It takes three years training at a school or college and another two years' apprenticeship in a salon; five years in all.

**How to train**
Special short course: as a guide I am quoting a popular course given in London (for men and women), by the London College of Fashion. Candidates should normally have reached GCE 'O' level standard.

The course provides instruction in ladies' and men's hairdressing, wig-making, make-up, manicure and pedicure together with design and general further education studies. Students completing the course satisfactorily will be eligible for the award of a College Certificate in Hairdressing. You should find your local Adult Education College will also provide similar courses qualifying you for the necessary City and Guilds Hairdressing Certificates.

There are many part-time day and evening courses. Remember that extra study and qualifications is necessary to do any hair tinting. Do not attempt it otherwise.

**Equipment**
You could possibly buy a secondhand hair-drier from £20 upwards. I am told that it is considered 'old hat' to use hood-dryers. Customers prefer a quick-drying hand-drier (£10 or less secondhand).

Look for your equipment in journals like the *Hairdressers Journal*. Buy your shampoos, perm equipment, etc from wholesalers.

Unless you always work at home you will need a car with a boot large enough to carry your hair-drier and accessories. Buy a supply of extra towels in an open market at cut prices.

**Premises**
Be discreet. Hairdressing salons which have to pay big overheads are very jealous of freelancers and may complain if you take business away from them. You will need constant hot water in your bathroom and access to a nearby launderette if you do not have a washing machine for your towels. You will need at least 30 to 40 towels a week if you have a sufficient business to give you a good income.

**Write to**
Your local School or College of Hairdressing for evening classes and training in tinting with real models (you can sometimes get your own hair done free by offering yourself as a model). (See *Useful Contacts*).

**Law**

Get advice from C.A.B. if you find your business is growing too fast; you may also have to check with your landlord as well. It is safer for you to divide your appointments equally between home and outside visits.

**Advertising**

This is much better left to personal recommendation and a build-up of connections among local friends and acquaintances.

**What you can earn**

Charges should be kept competitive with local shops and salons, therefore the amount charged will vary considerably – depending on your area.

**Advantages**

Many clients will prefer your individual attention to the open-plan system of most salons. There's nothing routine about the variety of people you meet.

**Disadvantages**

If it is to be a successful business you may well have to put personal plans to one side to deal with emergencies. Clients are bound to expect refreshments on the house.

## *Home Economist*  M/F  25–60

The Home Economist is a professional adviser on food, nutrition, textiles, clothing, home management and design, household services and research related to the home and community. The Home Economist's work may include demonstrations and lectures, recipe development, product testing and the preparation of food for photography, TV etc. With Dietetic qualifications, there are opportunities to prepare diets for manufacturers, magazines and the public. Freelance Home Economists often employ intelligent housewives with some experience to help them with secretarial and research work.

**Training**

You must take a course which is recognised for full membership of the Association of Home Economics. The Certificate course, duration 2 years, is the shortest. To enter you need four GCE 'O' levels (or recognised equivalent) including English, English Literature or History. There are approximately 24 colleges throughout the country offering this certificate course.

**Equipment**

The normal secretarial equipment.

**Premises**

You can work at home or from home. There are openings for freelance home economists. And it is easier to start if contacts made during full time employment can be built on. However, it is possible to start from scratch, but it is that much harder to get off the ground.

**Write to**

The Freelance Agency H.E.R. 25 Fitzjohn's House, 46 Fitzjohn's Avenue, Hampstead, London NW3 5LU also to The Secretary, Association of Home Economists Ltd, 192–198 Vauxhall Bridge Road, London SW1X 1DX (Tel: 01-821 6421). The Association has a freelance list for its members covering the country which it sends to all employers who ask for it.

**Law**

No restrictions.

**Advertising**

There is no bar against home economists advertising themselves, but there is no recognised place where employers might look for them.

**What you can earn**

The Secretary of the Association of Home Economists says: 'I freelance myself as a consultant and my income varies tremendously according to who employs me!' But it would be a fair guide to say that £3 an hour is the minimum with any expenses on top paid by the employer or £30 a day rising with experience.

### Advantages
Currently freelance jobs are on the increase, as many firms are realising that in hard times the home economist's contribution is important, but do not have the money to initiate a home economics department or to employ a home economist full time.

### Disadvantages
You must study hard to qualify.

---

## Home Minding Help   M/F   15–50

No investment required. Fair to good income. Can be done at home, partly at home, from home or close to your home. This work has boomed rapidly in the past few years, owing to the increase in house-burglary, with resultant damage to property, violation, vandalism and loss. The need for home minders as a protection against burglars and vandals is just as great in small towns and villages as it is in large towns and cities, in rural areas and city blocks of flats as in housing estates and semi-detached homes that are left unprotected during holiday periods.

The idea is possibly to form your own agency to provide home minders via a working shift system in which you can also take part if and when necessary, or to 'mind other people's property' such as jewellery, small items of furniture or clothing, paintings, furs etc., in your own home, while the owners are absent or abroad on holiday or business.

### Qualifications
Health and strength; an unimpeachable reputation. Some mechanical ability or karate training. Courage!

### Training
At a keep fit class; some knowledge of first aid would be useful. You could ask to be apprenticed for a short period to one of the many Security Firms in your area. Consult your local police station and Fire Prevention Service.

### Equipment
A car helpful but not strictly essential. Motorcycle or bicycle. A torch, notebook, gloves. You can sometimes find pre-war lightweight policemen's truncheons on sale at jumble sales where they are offered as valued antiques. Take out an extra insurance policy (see below).

### Premises
You must have your own telephone. Get permission from the police and your Local Authority. (Remember you must get a licence to run an agency, cost £108 per annum.)

### Write to
The Home Office and Head Office of your County Police and Local Police Inspector. Your own solicitor re your new agency and/or security work. Then write to the Editor of your local paper and to your local radio station or to the BBC.

### Advertising
Keep an 'ad' in your local paper and magazines; cards in newsagents' windows.

### What you can earn
Ask for an interview with your nearest Private Detective Agency to ask what you should charge. Your fee should relate to the value of the property you have to guard. Also you must charge for your fares, transport, expenses, unsociable hours.

**Advantages**

If you are among the first people to think of starting such an Agency to provide Home-minders in your town, city or village, you are certain of some good business. (Two more house-burglaries will have taken place during the time it takes me to type this paragraph.) Burglars are said to study newspaper columns for funerals, weddings etc., so they know when a house is likely to be empty and ripe for. 'plucking' so you too have a first class guide as to where and when you should look for your clients.

**Disadvantages**

You may find it more difficult or expensive to obtain a Life Insurance Policy for yourself. In any case, take out a special 'Home-minders' insurance policy and ask the local police whether it is okay for you to arm yourself with an antique truncheon from a jumble sale.

## *Home shopper*  M/F  18–70

Agent for mail order companies. No investment. Small earner can be done close to your home.

**Qualifications**

Health and strength; plenty of friends and neighbours.

**Training**

None required. I obtained advice on mail order selling from: John Moores Home-shopping Service, Kershaw Avenue, Crosby, Liverpool XL70 1AB (Littlewoods Mail Order Stores Ltd). They tell me: 'Finding customers is a matter of an individual's situation. In our experience most agents start with members of their own family as customers. They add on to these close friends and near neighbours and then, as word spreads, they will have been approached by friends of friends, etc. Although there are no firm figures available, we would say that an average agent has between five and ten regular customers.' (This information comes from Mrs P. H. L. Goodchild, P.R. Department, 11th Floor, J.M. Centre, Old Hall Street, Liverpool XL70 1AB.)

**Equipment**

A car would help but is not essential; a telephone would be useful too. Stationery is provided.

**Premises**

This would not really suit an isolated household, unless part of a large family, as you need a fair number of neighbours.

**Write to**

If you are over the age of 18, you can write to the company of your choice and ask for the necessary application forms (or you can complete and return one of the reply coupons which appear in advertisements in magazines and newspapers very frequently).

**Law**

No restrictions; must be over 18.

**Advertising**

Watch the newspapers and magazines advertisements for coupons; you advertise yourself by word of mouth.

**What you can earn**

Mail order houses pay commission to their agents based on the amount of payments collected from customers and sent into the company. The normal rate of this commission at present is 10p in the £ in cash, 12½p in the £ if the commission is taken in goods. From this you will see that the amount of earnings possible depends largely on the number of customers and the amount of business.

**Advantages**

Catalogue mail order has grown

rapidly in the past ten years as an alternative form of shopping and in 1980 total sales for the industry will top £2,500 million. Major benefits are credit, commission, convenience and social contacts. However, increasing (and high) postal charges may have affected it adversely.

**Disadvantages**
It can sometimes be difficult selling to friends.

## Host family (1)   M/F   12–90

Minimal investment. Good income. Can only be done at home.

**Qualifications**
This is best done through an approved agency. You will need to provide a holiday home for young people or foreign guests. This means providing hospitality as well as accommodation and usually means 'a homely atmosphere' for the summer holidays. You may have to provide a photograph of your own family and the house or district, plus a description of the facilities, and locality and a few remarks; details of the host's profession, his wife's age, ages of any children and so on. This enables an agency to match children to the host family's background.

**Training**
Study the leaflets and brochures provided by a number of agencies throughout Britain who arrange these visits. If you have children of your own it's a help. Also consult the various agencies about children's tastes and the studies and interests of foreign guests.

**Premises**
Necessary accommodation: a warm, pleasant vacant room at home also required (sometimes) are the availability of churches or local tuition in English language, sport and so on.

**Write to**
En Famille Agency, Westbury House, Queens Lane, Arundel, Sussex (Tel: Arundel (0903) 882450; Telegrams: Enfam, Arundel.) This agency caters for the whole of England and also has some host families in Ireland, Scotland and Wales. They tell me: 'However, because of the popularity of the area the majority of our families live in southern England including the West Country.'

Also, write to the Guide Activities Department, London Transport Board, 26 Grosvenor Gardens, London SW1 (Tel: 01-730 3450), and your Local Tourist Office.

**Law**
An agency will expect you to give references from two people of standing e.g., solicitor, magistrate, church official, doctor, school or college official.

**Advertising**
Watch the newsagents' window in your local area, and school or youth magazines. Many south-east towns and villages newsagents' windows throughout the spring and summer carry these cards put there by the agencies, schools and private persons offering or asking for such accommodation.

**What you can earn**
The E.F.A. says that in 1981 in Britain families can expect to receive from £42 per week up to £75 per week for full board. The lowest terms are for ordinary comfortable homes with no claim to luxury amenities. Highest are for accommodation and board of extremely high quality and/or extras, such as a tennis court, swimming pool, stables with horses etc.

Cost of excursions, outings, and/or

44

pocket money should be discussed beforehand.

**Advantages**
If you have children of a similar age, they have the chance to brush up their knowledge of a foreign language; al-

though the object of course is for the visitor to learn English.

**Disadvantages**
You can never be sure what you're going to get.

# Host family (2)  M/F  25–65

No investment needed.

This work is offered by Local Councils to any person or families who act as hosts to usually an older person in need of a rest or holiday.

**Qualifications**
A kind heart, comfortable home; if possible some experience of living with an elderly person but not strictly necessary.

**Training**
Not needed.

**Equipment**
Your own home, with a cosy spare room and bed.

**Premises**
As above.

**Write to**
Head of Social Services Department at

your Town Hall. Also write to Mrs Sheila Wicks or to Deputy Director of Social Services Department, Surrey House, 34 Eden Street, Kingston-upon-Thames.

Write also to: Mrs Gillian Noon, Church Road, Ashford, Middlesex.

**Law**
Does not apply, but you should inform your own Doctor that you are doing this work under a Local Authority scheme called 'Sharing the Caring'.

**Advertising**
Does not apply.

**What you can earn**
Present rate of payment is about £40 per week.

**Advantages**
A worthwhile job and some profit.

# Housewife's shopping driver  M/F  25–55

No investment if you have your own motorcar in roadworthy condition. The Government hopes you will not be so naughty as to make a big profit. (See comments below.) The Ministry of Transport have issued a booklet saying in effect that if you use your own car like taxi-hire, especially in rural areas, you are showing really public-spirited common sense. Can be done from home.

**Qualifications**
Clean driving licence; good, reliable

driving; an ability to park the car skilfully in busy High Streets.

**Training**
Some years of driving in all weather and road conditions.

**Equipment**
Always carry a spare tyre, cheque book, credit or bank cards, driving licence, insurance policy; be AA or RAC registered if possible. You need a car with a large boot or space to carry neighbour's shopping. Check every

few days on petrol, oil, tyres, batteries, water, clean plugs etc.

## Premises
A good idea in rural districts with none or few buses is for housewife shoppers to meet at your house so that you can start together in good order and discuss who pays for what and how much. You can check the shops to which people want to be taken; find out where they want to be collected. For small *extra* payments you deliver them with their parcels to their own doorsteps. (This experiment began in rural districts of the north-east where it is highly successful, though expensive to run.)

## Write to
Put up a notice in your local doctors' surgery or clinic, in the village hall or church, giving dates when you plan to drive to town; give your phone number.

## Law
Ministry of Transport say no extra insurance needed. (Only their blessing apparently!), but it would be wise to check with your Insurance Company and inform them. Make sure you know by heart every sign and word of the Highway Code.

## Advertising
Mr Norman Fowler, the Minister of Transport, says you can!

## What you can earn
I shall quote what the Minister thinks you should earn for this job. As a driver, in my opinion, his figures are far too low. I suggest you fix your own. Here are the prices recommended by the Minister. At Spring 1980 prices, costs for a medium-sized saloon (1600 cc) per mile, could be charged at 4½p petrol, 4½p oil, service/repairs, totalling 9p per mile; 7p for a small (1000 cc) car. The Ministry of Transport Instruction says: 'Driver may of course reasonably charge the *entire* cost of a journey to a passenger if they themselves would not have otherwise taken the journey.'

## Advantages
They're almost too obvious for all concerned.

## Disadvantages
You are limited to a car with not more than eight seats. I don't really fancy eight back-seat drivers!

# Indexer   M/F   25–50

Low investment, medium to good income. Can be done at home, though you will possibly have to meet your clients at their offices, and the majority of publishers are based in London.

## Qualifications
A good education, ability to spell well, tidy and methodical mind and habits, typing ability, willingness to follow a brief and a training in indexing.

## Training
A library background could be helpful. The Rapid Results College has established a correspondence course which gives a sound and comprehensive introduction to the principles and techniques of indexing; it currently costs £59 and would take between three and six months to complete depending on how much time you devote to it.

## How to train
Take a course such as that mentioned above, and study books on indexing. Practise indexing.

## Equipment
Your own typewriter, pens, pencils, index cards, typing paper, index boxes for bigger jobs, rubber bands etc. Reference books. After your permanent

items have been bought the main recurring expense will be new index cards.

## Premises
Any room at home with a table for typing and for sorting out your cards. You will need good lighting (both during the day and for evening work) so as not to strain your eyes, and a comfortable level of heating as it is a mainly sedentary occupation. A small room for your own study is the ideal; if you have to work in the living room, train your family to leave your things alone.

## Write to
The Rapid Results College, 27/37 St George's Road, London SW19 4DS (Tel: 01-947 2211).

Also if you are serious contact the Society of Indexers at 7a Parker Street, Cambridge CB1 1JL (Tel: Cambridge (0223) 311913.) Remember to enclose a large stamped-addressed envelope.

## The Society of Indexers
This was founded in 1957 to safeguard and promote indexing standards and the professional interests of indexers. There are now members in many overseas countries, including a substantial membership in Australia. The American Society of Indexers, covering the USA and Canada, was founded in 1969 and has been affiliated to the Society since 1971.

Any individual or any corporate body with an interest in indexing is eligible for membership of the Society. The subscription is £10 payable in advance on 1st April each year. Any new member enrolled between 1st January and 30th April is required to pay only half this amount for the remaining part of the membership year.

The Society, which rightly insists that indexing is not something that everyone can do, publishes its own journal, *The Indexer*; it comes out twice a year, in April and October, and each member receives a free copy. This is the only journal in the field of Indexing; it is also the journal of the American Society.

It was at the insistence of the Society and with the co-operation of some of its members, that the course mentioned in *Training* was established; it is now run entirely by the College, the Society's continued interest being confined to professional and academic consultation.

The Society is administered entirely on an honorary basis, but it aims to reply helpfully to call enquiries and requests from its members, as well as from publishers and others who commission indexes. It also maintains a specialist collection of books and other publications on indexing. This is housed in the Library Association's library at 7 Ridgmount Street, London WC1.

## Register of Indexers
Any member who has completed at least one index, published or unpublished (in addition to any indexing exercises forming part of a training course) and satisfactorily answers the Society's questionnaire, which tests knowledge and techniques, may apply for recognition as a Registered Indexer. Members who are admitted to the Society's Register are nominated to publishers and others who seek the Society's help in commissioning indexes. Application forms and full details are available from the Secretary.

## Members' Meetings
Indexing can be a lonely job if you are doing it all the time, and so the Society encourages its members to maintain contact with each other, and to form local groups. It holds general meetings and a national conference in London, where there are also discussion evenings and occasional lectures for those who live within travelling distances.

## Law
No legal restrictions. However, indexers are paid an outright fee for their

contribution to a book; the publishers are deemed to have copyright and therefore there is no extra payment when the book is reprinted or goes into paperback, unless (which is very rare) a specific agreement is made to the contrary.

## Advertising

Through trade journals; the *Bookseller*, *Times Literary Supplement*, and the *Times Educational Supplement*. However, you will probably find that word of mouth and personal recommendation is more useful, particularly if you are not on the Society of Indexers' Register.

Try to get your name on to an agency's books; consult the *Writer's and Artist's Yearbook* in your local public library to find them.

## What you can earn

Payment varies immensely, depending on the length of a job, its difficulty, how much work you have to put into it. As a very rough guide current rates are around £3.50 an hour. Payment can be by the hour, by the number of entries, or you might prefer to negotiate a flat fee.

## Advantages

For a typewriter owner there is very little investment, because of the small amount of equipment you need. It is clean, quiet work; and you don't need strong arms, or a great deal of manual dexterity.

## Disadvantages

Publishers always want indexes in a hurry, but are not always so keen to pay you for your work in a hurry. Working under great pressure can be very exhausting.

It is not a job to be lightly undertaken; you will find it very difficult to obtain repeat orders if you ever turn in an index that is slipshod, and so you must maintain a high standard of work. It is *not* easy to get work unless you already have contacts within the world of publishing. You must enjoy working largely on your own and be very familiar with reference books.

The aim of the Society of Indexers include (among other) advising on the qualifications of indexers, and raising their status; you have got to be *good*.

## *Journalist* M/F 16–60

No investment (except your own tough constitution). Can be very high income. Can be done at or from home.

## Qualifications

Experience. Few people realise how simple it is to become a journalist, especially if you are active and resilient. You need cheek and nerve. (Some of our best newspaper reporters started as office-boys or inquisitive typists.) Some education needed, but not much! You must be able to type, quickly, even if it's with one finger. Shorthand does help.

## Training

Call (do not write or phone) on the News Editor of your smallest local daily or evening paper. (A weekly paper is even better.) If he throws you out, go back a week later. Repeat, until he says okay you can do a week's work and see what happens.

If you are a female dress very dashingly. If you are male, dress very dashingly. Invite the News Editor to go with you to the nearest pub for a drink, unless you are under age. If you call to see him *with* a story, your chances are much better. The 'story' can be a bit of local gossip. It doesn't matter how small the story provided it is absolutely, totally *new* and no one else knows about it.

Another way to persuade the News

Editor to give you trials is to give him some gossip about the local football or cricket team. Meanwhile spend all your spare time in the local Magistrates Court just listening to cases. Get to know the police.

If you live in a large town, it would be useless to adopt this method of entering the profession by going to the 'big' paper (e.g. *Birmingham Post* or *Yorkshire Post*). They would not give any inexperienced person a trial. It must be a *small* paper circulating in a suburb or rural area.

## How to train
Stay with the job you are given for at least six months; then go to the nearest News Agency (you will find them all listed in the *Writers' and Artists' Yearbook* in your local library) and work perhaps a year there. Then try a larger paper.

## Equipment
A pair of good feet; typewriter if possible; telephone certainly, a car an advantage but not a necessity. The best advice I can give the married woman journalist who wants to freelance from home is to have some babies and write all about it for the press. Later write about housework and become 'Superwoman'.

## Premises
Work at home. The Editor doesn't want to see you kicking your heels about the office. Keep away; but always leave the News Editor's secretary a message or telephone number where you can instantly be found.

## Write to
If you have a friend on a paper, write and ask if any vacancies are likely to occur. Apart from this, don't write to anybody. The only writing for you now is writing for some rag, paper magazine, broadcast journal or agency and remember you expect to be paid for it too . . . so much per 1,000 words. Remember letters-to-the-Editor are *not*

paid for – so don't. The address of the National Council for the Training of Journalists, is Carlton House, Hemnall Street, Epping, Essex, CM16 4NL.

## Law
The snag is not getting into journalism but getting into the Union. You cannot work for a paper until you are a member of the National Union of Journalists (except, of course, as trainee-probationer) and you can't become a member until you're a journalist. But you can become a freelance member of the Freelance Branch of the N.U.J. if you can show you're earning a living wage by your freelance work. Cost of probationary membership went up in 1980 to £32 per annum.

## Advertising
On the whole advertisements are distrusted by journalists, possibly because the press resents being dependent on advertising. An ad in a trade paper like the *U.K. Press Gazette* might help.

## What you can earn
Staff work is highly paid. However, without a Trade Union card of the N.U.J. (National Union of Journalists) it is unlikely that any work would be accepted. Freelance writing for a specialists magazine can, however, qualify you for membership of the Union eventually if you do enough of it. It depends only on how much work you can get accepted and how much you earn per annum. For example, if you are a newcomer to the business, you would need to earn between £1,000 and £1,500 a year to qualify. Suppose, for example, that you wrote articles on cookery or specialist diets – if these became well known and received sufficient publicity, this could enable you in due course to apply to join the Union (after a probationary period of one to two years).

Rates of pay vary from the extremely small, possibly £15 or £20 an 800-word article in a minor magazine (e.g.

specialising in holiday articles, health or hobby concerns) to between £35 or £100 for a 1200-word article in a newspaper. A provincial paper would pay £15 to £20 for an article by someone obscure whereas a sum between £50 and £100 or more would be paid (since inflation to say, a well known doctor or Member of Parliament. The most lucrative articles are those which make a series of one, two to four articles, such as those featured in Sunday papers. The price would vary according to subject between £200 and £2,000 or more. Non-journalists, however, can earn 'tip-off' money without writing a single line. These are usually gossip items, sport news or 'scandal'; if you knew about some irregularity in a hospital (or of some possibly 'heroic' figure in such a place) you would be welcome to visit any local News Editor and give information in strict confidence. Depending on the news value the price would range from £5 to £50 or much more.

You could work up a connection with your local evening or weekly newspaper if you have some specialist knowledge. It could be sport, chess, dancing competitions, local theatre or amateur theatricals, local charity or pop concerts. You can write to the Editor or to someone on the staff whose name you have seen bylined in the paper and ask if you may call. A telephone call is more popular if you are shy, a visit is recommended; you should ask to speak to the Secretary of the News Editor, Sports Editor or the Editor himself unless it is a big paper when he is too grand for this kind of approach. You will be asked to send in a few hundred words of 'copy' (not more than 500 words for an evening paper) and if this is published, you are 'in'. After that any further material from you would be welcome, if you always telephone first and ask whether you may write about a particular local event. This is often welcome to the editorial staff because it frees a man or woman to concentrate on some other story. Freelances do not normally get expenses unless it is a 'big' story, but you can send a little note of bus fares or train fares, telephone calls and so on. Newspapers pay from about 13p to 15p a mile for petrol, according to the make of your car. Hotel bills must be kept and sent to the cashier.

**Advantages**
A married woman with a family – if she is already an experienced journalist (even if only on some small local 'rag') can earn an excellent living with just her typewriter and telephone. If she is wise she will exploit her own family, writing about her experiences of love, pregnancy, married life. . . .

**Disadvantages**
Your family may not like being in the paper.

---

## *Junk restoreer*   M/F   16–60 (*see below under Training*)

No investment. Good profit when learned.

**Qualifications**
None but willingness to learn how to mend junk, i.e. you will be shown how to restore to perfect working order as good as new, thrown-out vacuum-cleaners, washing machines, TV-sets, radios, electric irons, kettles, toasters, cookers etc. When mended, the goods are put on sale in the window of your local 'Brass Tacks' (see below).

**Training**
To find out if you are the right age

group to be eligible, try the Youth Opportunities Programme (Y.O.P.) if 16–18 or your local Manpower Services Commission (M.S.C.) if 19–24. If older you are still eligible if out of work six months or a year.

## Equipment
Not required, but take your own tools along.

## Premises
After a period of training, work at home.

## Write to
Your Local Project Manager. For London Area try Mr Robin Dean, Project Manager, 18 Ashwin Street, Dalston London E8. Also try Area (North of Thames) Manager Mr A. E. Jones, (Tel: 01-632 5316), or (South) Mr W. E. Jackson (Tel: 01-632 5314). Or try Director, Marian Rigge of the Mutual Aid Centre (Tel: 01-980 6263). Look in your local phone book for Manpower Services Commission, and for the Youth Opportunities Programme.

## Law
No restrictions.

## Advertising
Advertise your services wherever you like, window-card, newsagents card.

## What you can earn
Robin Dean of 'Brass Tacks' (see *Useful Contacts*) says: 'We ask what we think is a reasonable price considering the area. We try to have on show both expensive stuff and cheap stuff.'

## Advantages
Once you've learned the trick, you could start a business connection without much trouble, considering that ordinary housewives cannot find an electrician or electrical repairman for love nor money.

## Disadvantages
You may get a shock (not electric) when you actually realise that your mended goods are often better quality than newer makes.

---

# Kleeneze sales person  M/F  25–45

---

This particular firm send out circulars explaining their kind of selling and what they have to offer; they invite you to write to them to learn more about it. The work is sometimes advertised in magazines and newspapers. Can be done at home.

## Qualifications
Gift of the gab, it's called, to persuade other people to buy.

## Training
The Kleeneze firm give you some instruction but no training is required.

## Equipment
You have to lay out £7.50 to cover the cost of a small case of demonstration products. This fee also includes the first of a regular monthly bulletin giving selling tips and news of new products. Stock is brought from the local distributor each week at 30% discount. An urban or suburban environment is essential if travelling expenses are to be kept to a minimum.

## Premises
Kleeneze say that working from home can be built up into a family business.

## Write to
Messrs Kleeneze Ltd, Ansteys Road, Hanham, Bristol, BS15 3DY (Tel: Bristol (0272) 670861).

**Law**
No restrictions. Kleeneze is a reputable firm, but before paying your £7.50 to do this kind of trading, it is a good idea to call in at your local C.A.B. office and tell them your intentions. Ask their advice before sending off your money.

**What you can earn**
The firm say (I quote them): 'An hour's work a day could average total sales of £10 in 5 days – yielding £3 profit. Also there are ample opportunities for earning refunds additional to the basic discount.'

**Advantages**
It *sounds* an easy way of making money. But don't sign any contracts until you see whether you like it or not. Kleeneze products are well made and last well.

**Disadvantages**
The jobs that sound easy very often aren't.

## *Knitter* M/F 21–75

Investment can be pricey if you decide to buy a knitting machine. Investment can be equally low by *not* buying one. Income is modest unless you specialise or have special skills. Can be done at home.

**Qualifications**
You must be able to knit or crochet a garment with a correct and even tension; correct measurements; accuracy in following the pattern and the work must look clean and neat.

**Training**
Manufacturers whom you approach will ask you to send in a new sample garment made in the firm's own wool, with a variety of stitches so that they can test your work.

**How to train**
Try sending a sample of your work, a 3-inch square in stocking stitch in 2 ply or finer wool to a manufacturer or yarn spinner whose name you can choose from a list of such addresses in the *Branded Textile Merchandise and Trade Marks Directory* which you can find in most large public libraries. Get advice from the Wool Secretariat, Wool House, Carlton House Gardens, London SW1 (Tel: 01-930 7300). Also from the Public Relations Officer, Shelley Stewart, at Courtaulds Headquarters, London.

**Equipment**
Only if and when you can build up a faithful network of reliable customers is it sensible to think about buying a knitting machine. For example, Knitmaster Ltd, 30–40 Elcho Street, London SW1 (Tel: 01-228 9303) insist that they do *not* buy any knitting work whatsoever. They only sell the machines. In their advertisements Knitmaster claim that garments are so easy to knit and produce such attractive patterns that a *few* Knitmaster owners who have designing ability do have considerable success in selling their work to boutiques. Knitmaster tell me 'what we do emphasise is the fact that hundreds of women owning our machines do earn varying incomes – some of them small and some quite considerable – by selling garments which they knit.' (Some articles in women's magazines have unfortunately given the impression that firms selling the machines also buy the goods. This is an error. If you invest in a machine you still have to sell your stuff yourself. So think twice about investing in a machine.)

**Premises**
You will need a good working table in your own sitting room or kitchen.

**Write to**
Your nearest shops and manufacturers. Baby clothes and maternity

shops are good customers. Knitmaster (address above) are keen to give advice and instruction and inspect your samples.

Jean Wiseman of Knitmaster recommends you join one of the hundreds of knitting clubs or start your own club. Also by wearing one of your own 'creations' in a pub or office, you get orders and start to build up a clientele.

### Law
There are no restrictions whatsoever. But C.A.B. offices throughout the country have specially asked that everyone should consult them first before purchasing any machines.

### Advertising
It depends where you live. If you live in a small village, then a card in the newsagents. Otherwise don't spend money on advertising. Write individual letters to shops, boutiques and manufacturers and try to build up a reliable connection to accept your work.

### What you can earn
The thinner the wool, the more intricate the pattern, the higher the earnings, some firms pay by the ounce so that a heavy double knit would also earn well.

I am told by many knitting friends that earnings with an electric machine are high and that £10 per hour is by no means impossibly high, BUT only for women determined to do it as a full-time business and spend time and effort finding customers also.

### Advantages
Most people can knit.

### Disadvantages
That's why this one is unlikely to make your fortune.

## Lampshade-maker   M/F   18–60

Very small investment. Steady to excellent income as your speed and efficiency improve. Can be done entirely at home.

### Qualifications and training
Nimble fingers, some sewing ability. Train at evening or day classes, which are advertised in local papers, at your Town Hall, Post Office and library. In some villages people drop leaflets through your door about classes for various crafts, including lampshade-making, run by Adult and Community Education Centres at the local school or village hall.

You first learn to produce simple types of 'soft' lampshade. (The Trade have two types – soft and hard – soft are the easy ones to learn.) Later in the course you progress to the swirled, pleated, gathered and hard types.

Some lampshade factories send an experienced woman to your home for a number of days to train you. Some people are able to teach themselves by studying books. Two you could possibly get from your public Library are *Lampshades, Simple and Advanced* by Rourke, published Mills and Boon, price 60p and *Lampshades to Make* by E. Doeser, published Marshall Cavendish, price £2.50.

### Equipment
Glue, scissors and a Stanley knife, also a sewing-machine (secondhand). Use cheap taffeta for soft lampshades and even for lining, or buy Thai silks and exotic materials to stretch over a wire frame. Get wire frames from your local Crafts shop or big London stores like John Lewis. For hard lampshades, you can get fabric laminated to a stiffening agent. You also need templates made from quarter-inch formica or hardboard, against which you cut out the shapes. (Factories use special machinery to cut a large quantity at a time.)

### Premises
Use your bedroom floor or anywhere

in your home with room to cut out. Cut them out on a sheet of hardboard or formica but *not* on your carpet . . .

**Write to**
Your nearest lampshade-factory. Go round with your samples to gift shops and electrical shops.

**Law**
No restrictions but do contact your local C.A.B. before accepting any orders. They will check with the relevant trade union to see you are being paid enough for your work.

**Advertising**
Put an 'ad' in your local paper or try dropping a card through the letterbox of people who have just moved into new houses.

**What you can earn**
Factories reckon you make between £1.50 and £2.00 per hour when you are quick at it. You will make more money probably marketing your own work.

Lampshades sell for a lot of money – especially when made of unusual materials – look in the shops to observe the fashions and ask shopkeepers which types sell best. Standard lampshades sell now for about £25.

You will make an average of seven per day, rising to 10 when efficient, but it is best not to do a *whole* lampshade in one go – cut out a number and do one stage of the work on all of them one day, such as binding the wire. Next day you would pin, pull and stretch to make them really taut; stitch and glue them the following day, so that in a full week, you could produce about 35–40.

**Advantages**
It is independent sort of work where you can also use your own taste and imagination . . . and listen to the radio while you work.

**Disadvantages**
It can make your hands sore and your fingers ache!

## *Leather Worker*   M/F   16–60

### *(including Basket-making, Leather repair, Saddlery, etc.)*

Some investment on equipment, modest income. Can be done at home.

**Qualifications**
This work is another branch of *Craft Work* (see page 000), so you need the same talents as for needlework, art, etc.

**Training**
The W.I. courses are excellent. Get complete brochure from W.I. Books Limited (the National Federation of Women's Institutes), with a copy of their newest price-list from 39 Eccleston Street, Victoria, London, SW1W 9NT (Tel: 01-730 7212). Also get programme for training on all courses in leather crafts from Field Studies Council, Preston Montford, Montford Bridge, Shrewsbury, who run a 4-day course at £35 per person. They run 380 different craft courses at nine residential field centres throughout the country. Get details of other short courses from the National Institute of Adult Education, 19b De Montfort Street, Leicester, LE1 7GE. (See *Useful Contacts* for more courses, also prices for W.I. courses.)

For details of basket-making, try the Cane Centre, Jacobs, Young and Westbury Limited, Bridge Road, Haywards Heath, Sussex. (Tel: Haywards Heath (0444) 412411).

### How to train
Useful courses starting Spring 1981 on cane-seating, upholstery, etc. will also include other practical crafts such as picture-framing, furniture restoring, etc., will be held at Styal Workshop, Quarry Bank Mill, Styal, Cheshire, SK9 4LA (send a self-addressed and stamped envelope for the prospectus). Also at the Earnley Concourse (a residential Centre run by a Trust), with fees calculated on the number of nights you stay at Earnley. Two days cost £9, plus £9.20 for double bedroom per night per person or £11 for single room. Brochure (send s.a.e.) from the Earnley Concourse, near Chichester, Sussex, PO20 7JL. Get hold of *Cane-work* by Chas. Crampton, published Dryad Press, Leicester.

### Equipment
Sewing-machine, pattern, needles, glovers, tape measure, pencil, ruler, thimble, sharp pair of scissors, beeswax and thread. For basket-work: cane at about £12 per kilo, willow, shears, wooden-hinged ruler, bodkins, round-nosed pliers, picking knife, wrapping iron, screw-block all obtainable from 'Swinnertons', Ambercote, Stourbridge, near Birmingham.

### Premises
Work at home but you need a large room you can give over to it.

### Law
No restrictions.

### Advertising
Advertise in magazines and news-agents' windows; exhibit at galleries.

### What you can earn
You could charge for making a dog basket in four different sizes (average dog like a cocker spaniel) £4.75–£5.50; for a shopping basket, from about £4. To cane or rush chair, you could charge from £10 to £30 (reckon your work at £2.50 per hour, estimating about 15–20p per hole for an average dining chair containing 60–80 holes).

For leather work, you should fix your prices by examining work in galleries and shops, but the high cost of leather even when bought wholesale from your local tannery means you must charge quite high prices to cover expenses. Articles such as suede belts (which used to be profitable to make four years ago) now sell at £1 each in open markets because they are mass-produced.

### Advantages
All work which can be done entirely at home.

### Disadvantages
Basket-work, which used to be undertaken by the Institute for the Blind, is now much less popular, which makes me wonder what the reasons could be.

---

## *Lip-reading teacher* M/F 25–60

---

Investment nearly nil (but you should be a teacher). High income per hour. Can be done in your own home, or visiting pupils.

### Qualifications
There are Institutes which train you without a degree; post-graduates do an extra year at University.

In any case, you need the ability to get on with people, to communicate, to be patient, to teach old people and, as one teacher told me, 'to be like an actress on stage, to communicate by gesture'.

### Training
Intensive study at an Institute or Adult Education Institute or School for the Deaf; or you can take lessons privately; some students attend evening class; others go to University.

## How to train
One year at University. Classes at the City Literary Institute, Centre for the Deaf, Keeley House, Keeley Street, London, WC2B 4BA (Tel: 01-242 9872–6). Classes organised by your Local Education Authority. Among many training courses, try Manchester Polytechnic, Hilton House, Hilton Street, Manchester.

## Equipment
A blackboard and chalk.

## Premises
At home: one comfortable room, possibly big enough for a class of several people.

## Write to
Your Local Authority. Also: Rosemary McCall, in charge of Audiology at Princess Alice Hospital, Eastbourne. She founded the organisation 'LINK', (a charity) in 1972 for teaching deaf people in short courses. The address of 'LINK' is 19 Hartfield Road, Eastbourne, East Sussex, BN21 2AR (Tel: Eastbourne (0323) 638230).

## Law
No restrictions.

## Advertising
You are allowed to put up notices or posters in any health clinic or doctor's surgery or elsewhere.

## What you can earn
I asked one Local Authority in Surrey and was told that a qualified teacher would be paid (approximately) about £4 per hour for teaching a class of three or four people to lip-read. However, Miss McCall, Organising Secretary of 'LINK', thinks that some Further Education Authorities might not approve of groups as small as four people.

## Advantages
It is satisfying work, teaching all ages.

## Disadvantages
It can be quite tiring too; you must count on doing at least one hour's preparation before each class.

---

# Marriage Bureau  M/F  30–70

Financial investment is practically nil to begin with. Income is good but not reliable, depending on the number of contacts you have or can make. Can be done at home and by visiting clients.

## Qualifications
A sincere and sympathetic interest in human beings. A wide circle of friends, acquaintances. A face and voice that people can trust. Sophistication plus a good personal reputation. The ability to write a good letter.

## Training
It is a help if you have had some previous business training, either secretarial or agency work. Even more important is an interest in or some training in personal psychology. Experience in a

solicitor's office is the most helpful of all.

## How to train
Read books on marriage and marital relations. If possible, volunteer to work for a period as a marriage guidance counsellor in your locality. Study the advertisements in psychology journals and make a study of women's magazine columns of guidance on sex, love and romance.

You also need some background of foreign travel or experience in dealing with foreigners, because a substantial part of a modern marriage bureau's business attracts lonely foreigners and immigrants. This is a good way to start building up a connection. My hunch is that a marriage bureau run by a *man* could be a winner. 'Switch Agency' (see page 59) tried this two years ago, but gave up when they got too many women clients and not enough men!

## Equipment
Typewriter and good quality stationery, telephone, card index, access to a duplicating shop where you can have copies made of application forms, etc.

## Premises
A comfortable, inviting and impeccable sitting-room where you can not only invite applicants to call for interview, but where you could also arrange for partners to meet for the first time, with you as intermediary; thereby avoiding the embarrassment which applicants dread of going 'on a blind date'.

## Write to
Any local marriage bureau, asking for their application form so that you can see the sort of questions you must embody in your own application. There are no rules, however; you can have quite different questions if you wish. Also write to the National Council for Marriage Guidance, Herbert Gray College, Little Church Street, Rugby, Warwickshire (Tel: 0788 73241), and ask whether they have any advice or guidance.

## Law
It is advisable nowadays to register this business with your Local Authority. You should then be able to put on your letter-head 'Licensed by . . .'. However, consult the C.A.B. about this first.

You must also choose a name for your business and register it with the Registrar of Business Names (see *Useful Contacts*) for which you pay £1.

*Warning*: Marriage Bureaux are now liable to investigation under the Office of Fair Trading, so beware of troublemakers.

If you can afford it, also get a solicitor's advice on how to run your business.

## Advertising
Advertise in newspapers, magazines, newsagents, learned journals and in the more political magazines like the *New Statesman*, *The Spectator*, *New Society* etc. (Politicians and professors are often lonely people longing for love!)

## What you can earn
A typical registration fee in London today is £5 to get your name and details on to the bureau's books, or a membership fee of £55.00 for 12 months. Nowadays the fee is more often between £20 and £40 but it varies enormously. When a marriage is successfully arranged, a fee ranging from £25 to £100 can then be charged. It is up to you to charge a marriage-fee in accordance with the life-style of your clients. A reasonable sum would be between £30 and £40.

## Advantages
Obviously, there is a lot of job satisfaction in being the matchmaker if you are lucky enough to be able to bring happiness to your clients.

## Disadvantages
This is a business with a large element of gambling in it. Apart from the money, you will earn the undying gratitude of a few people and, in spite of all your skill and goodwill, cause bitter disappointment to many more.

You should know how to be discreet. Never gossip.

Medium to good income. High investment on training. Can be done at home or in nursery play groups.

This is a specialised method for training and educating young children based on a method devised by an Italian educationalist, Dr Maria Montessori, the first woman to qualify as a doctor at Rome University. As a doctor in an asylum in Rome between 1895 and 1900, she developed a method of educating defective or backward children which she afterwards applied to normal children also. It insists on spontaneity (as in 'liberal' kindergarten schools) and is opposed to rigid discipline, restrains or conventional rules. The method is explained in her books *The Montessori Method* and *The Secret of Childhood* (obtainable in English at libraries).

It requires the use of Montessori-trained teachers and special equipment, such as play-block, reading and other learning equipment.

Specially suited for a married woman (with a small child) who is interested in teaching – but is so far without a qualification – and who can find time to study and fit in lessons while still caring for her home and family.

### Qualifications and training

Diploma in the Montessori method of education. Good general education. To get the Diploma you must take a full-time (residential) course, Monday to Friday 9 a.m. to 4 p.m. or evening courses, Tuesday, Wednesday, Thursday 6 p.m. to 8 p.m. or courses by correspondence.

Students taking the full-time and evening Diploma courses study for a year of three terms (fee £800). The part-time course consists of three terms (£160, including enrolment). For the correspondence courses, course 1 cost £60 for U.K. and Ireland, overseas £85, and courses 2 and 3 £50 each. The examination fee is £30 or $70.

Those living too far from the Training Centre can study by correspondence course. Students have a tutor to whom they send their written work at regular intervals over a minimum period of 9 months. But all students are, if possible, expected to attend a two- or three-week vacation course before sitting for the examination for their Diploma. (Exams are also held in other cities besides London.)

### Equipment

Apparatus and books are obtainable from the Training Centre. A price list is issued.

### Premises

A suitable room at home.

### Write to

The Co-Principals, St Nicholas Training Centre for the Montessori Method of Education, 22–24 Princes Gate, London SW7 (Tel: 01-584 9232). The Co-Principal tells me: 'The St Nicholas Training Centre offers residence in three beautiful houses which overlook Hyde Park in front and a large secluded garden at the back.'

### Law

No restriction.

### Advertising

You can advertise yourself as a Montessori teacher in professional journals and elsewhere.

### What you can earn

I will quote the Co-Principal: 'Most of the women you are advising could find employment in nursery schools and playgroups. Working for the morning only they would probably earn about £20 per week. There are also mothers whose children have grown up and who have extra rooms in their homes who may decide to run their own nursery group. This can be very satisfying for anyone capable and really fond of children. Such women may also get work in local (independent) schools who need teachers for the youngest children. All-day teaching should be £35 to £40 per week.'

**Advantages**
You get a professional status for work always in demand.

**Disadvantages**
The high investment needed for training will deter many, but it is vocational work.

## *Mother's help*  M/F  18–50

Medium investment. Good to medium income. Can be done at home or close to your home.

It involves going to someone's house for an hour or a few hours when required to 'help out' with nursing, cooking, caring or babysitting. It involves cooperating with a local agency to do this work or you can join a group of friends and run the agency side of the business yourself; or you can take turns with your friends, i.e. sometimes you will run the agency and sometimes go out 'on call' to do the work or whatever is required.

**Qualifications and training**
Running your own home and family efficiently is the best possible qualification and training.

The idea is to start your own agency to help other housewives, who could be (though not necessarily) your neighbours and friends. To illustrate how it works, I shall quote a number of housewives who have done it and made a business success. Stopgap Services Ltd., Newlands, East End Road, Charlton Kings, Cheltenham, Glos. GL53 8QB (Tel: Cheltenham 37863). The directors, Mr and Mrs Shirley Roberts, said: 'We go to private homes to do nursing, night-duty or sleeping-in with a convalescent and we do home cooking, housework and shopping. This is usually a couple of hours per day. If the client wants his meal in the evening, we try to encourage him to have it mid-day so that the work can be done in school hours

when there are more helpers to select. Dinner parties are frequently prepared in the woman's home and taken to the client's house.

'Our girl recruits come from varied backgrounds and have varying qualifications. Most important is an attitude of mind to "have a go", general initiative and our ability to fit the girl to the job. We learn from our interview with her everything that the girl is prepared to do, and from her previous experience her capabilities. We get telephone calls almost daily from frustrated housebound women asking for help. Most of our clients come to us through recommendation.'

Two housewives at Oxted, Surrey decided to pool their resources, rented an office in the High Street, put an advertisement in the local paper and started their own business, an agency to find work (secretarial, bookkeeping, housekeeping) for 'mature ladies' in their district. They call themselves Switch Employment Agency, Station Road East, Oxted, Surrey (Tel: Oxted 2253/4). Business has grown considerably. They plan to extend 'operations' to home-minding and other jobs.

There are a number of such private agencies in the United Kingdom but not nearly enough of them. They provide help in shopping, packing, mending and running messages. In the London area there is Universal Aunts, 36 Walpole Street, London SW3 and Solve-your-Problem Ltd., 25a Kensington Church Street, London W8.

Follow their example and start your own agency.

## Equipment
Start simply with your own telephone at home, a pad and pencil, or link up with a friend or neighbour, and decide whose house you will use as your agency headquarters.

## Write to
Your nearest C.A.B. office and to your Local Authority. As a registered employment Agency, you must nowadays expect visits from a Government Inspector. Treat him or her as guide and friendly adviser.

## Law
You must now apply to your local Department of Employment for a Licence, cost approximately £108 per annum (introduced 1st August 1979). It will also involve visits from an Inspector at intervals.

## Advertising
One way to start is to have some cards printed and push them through letterboxes all round your district. Stopgap Services said: 'When we first started, we wrote to all schools, professional firms and businesses in Cheltenham and cold-canvassed a great many of them. We will send out our cards to every new firm starting in the town and reply to advertisements in the local evening paper, the *Gloucestershire*

*Echo*, but we do not now advertise for work – only for staff.'

## What you can earn
For the simpler jobs like shopping, packing, mending, running messages etc., the usual charge is now about £1 to £2 an hour. Clearly, the charges must vary according to the job and the number of hours spent on it and the qualifications of the woman you send on the job. You must also decide whether you will take a percentage of your staff's earnings or whether you will charge only the client. Some agencies do both; some prefer only to charge the client.

## Advantages
If you keep your overheads modest at the beginning, there is still a clear profit in this work, even if you keep your charges as low as possible.

## Disadvantages
Your head must rule your heart, or you and your staff may find yourselves being exploited.

## Comment
If business drops off in one line, do not be disheartened. Switch to something else! For instance, you could apply for a licence to sell secondhand clothing, and so have two strings to your bow. The demand for mother's help is terrific, especially if he or she is willing to do night-duty sometimes.

---

## *Motorcar repairer*  M/F  20–50

High investment. High income. Can be done at home, or outside your home. Can also be done from a mobile workshop in the client's own garage or drive, but then investment is higher.

## Qualifications
Some mechanical knowledge, and a thorough knowledge of cars and car manufacture.

## Training
Garage experience, minimum two years.

## How to train
Train in D.I.Y. Car Maintenance Centre, Milton Keynes. Ring 'Brass Tacks' (see *Useful Contacts*) for particulars. Evening classes at your Institute of Education or try tampering with

your own or your neighbour's car. Work full- or part-time in a maintenance garage or petrol-station.

## Equipment
It may cost you a total of £1,000 to £1,500 to buy the following basic equipment: hydraulic jack, vice, bench, ramp, a new box of tools (up to £500 just for this!) You may possibly have to dig a pit in your garage or yard floor. However, you could do minor jobs with less equipment.

The Local Authority may ask you to remove the piece of road kerb in front of your house, which could cost anything between £200 and £500.

## Premises
It would be useless to try getting permission to run your own car repair business if you live in a residential road in some gracious-looking suburb. Nor would you get permission, unless there is ample room in front of your house, or in your yard or garden.

## Write to
Your Local Authority and Planning Officer. Without their blessing, you can't go any further with this; that is, you could try but you'd never get away with it unless you live in the depths of the country.

## Law
The law is hard enough on motorists and I'm afraid it wouldn't be very nice to you either, if you didn't conform to all legal requirements. Consult the C.A.B.

## Advertising
The odd card in the newsagent won't do any harm. Personal recommendation is best.

## What you can earn
Quite a lot. My own car mechanic says he earns a good living, doing it outside his front gate in good weather. He uses a waterproof polythene sheet and earns more than working for a garage where the proprietor collects most of the money.

## Advantages
If you have a real talent for cars, people will flock to your door – hence the obstruction clause.

## Disadvantages
The sheer hardship of getting this business off the ground.

---

## *Mushroom grower*   M/F   20–45

---

High investment needed. Good income. Can be done at home, in your garden, yard or shed, even in a room.

## Qualifications
You need specialist knowledge obtained by reading and lectures.

## Training
The Mushroom Growers' Association, which is a specialist branch of the National Farmers' Union, publishes a monthly magazine (the *Mushroom Journal*) available to members only.

Cost of Associate Membership has now gone up to £50 plus V.A.T. (i.e. £57.50); this entitles you to receive each month a copy of the *Mushroom Journal* to keep you up-to-date with the mushroom world and the people in it.

The Mushroom Growers' Association suggests that before you start, you should read the book by F. C. Atkins called *Mushroom Growing Today*. The copies published by Faber are all sold out, so get it from your public library, or write to the M.G.A. Office at Agriculture House, Knightsbridge, London, SW1X 7NJ (Tel: 01-235 5077). The book gives all the relevant details as to what equipment and buildings you need.

### How to train

The Mushroom Growers' Association also arranges from time to time farm walks and meetings whereby growers can get together with mutual benefits. Farm walks consist of a tour of the host farm and after refreshments the owner usually answers questions on his method of growing. Sometimes special lectures are given. Meetings are arranged throughout the United Kingdom; there are also overseas tours.

### Equipment

See F. C. Atkins's book, as above.

### Premises

The Mushroom Growers' Association dislikes the idea that some people have of trying to grow mushrooms in a sack out in your garage or on a small patch of land in the garden; although this may be all right if you only want to grow mushrooms as a hobby, it is simply not a commercial proposition. You really need premises the size of a small factory or smallholding if possible – to be commercial.

### Write to

M.G.A. Headquarters, Agriculture House.

### Law

The Mushroom Growers' Association can arrange all kinds of insurances with the N.F.U. Mutual Insurance Society Ltd.

It also arranges legal advice (from the N.F.U.) for members and supports planning applications. If you start a mushroom farm, you will need planning permission.

### Advertising

Leave this to the M.G.A.

### What you can earn

Warning: the Association says that large growers have had financial difficulties lately; some have gone into liquidation and many farms have had to reduce their staff.

### Advantages

You'll be popular with mushroom-lovers among your friends!

### Disadvantages

That is, if you don't go broke (see above).

---

## Music teacher   M/F   22–65

No investment. Modest income. Can be done at home.

### Qualifications

You should be a qualified teacher of one or more instruments. To enter your pupils for the examinations of the Royal Schools of Music you must be qualified; but if you are (say) a good pianist you can teach the rudiments to tiny tots without formal qualifications. (see *Odd Jobs*).

### Training

A full-time 3-year course of study at one of the Colleges or Academies of Music.

### How to train

Student music teachers will learn modern methods of psychology, communication and teaching generally. They are also required to study an instrument additional to the piano.

Entry to a music college is usually by examination, and the successful student is awarded a diploma after taking the final examinations.

### Equipment

A piano or other instrument in good condition; music stand for other instruments, sheet music (your pupils will pay for any you buy for them).

### Premises
A warm room at home, large enough to take a piano.

### Write to
The Royal College of Music, The Royal Academy of Music, or The Trinity College of Music, or your local College, to get details of courses and examinations.

Also write to: Mr Norman Hearn, The Director, Rural Music Schools Association, Little Benslow Hills, Hitchin, Herts, SG4 9RB (Tel: Hitchin 59446). This school now runs a course, open to all adults. The annual subscription is currently £5, £8 for two members (it is a registered charity). The President is Mr Norman Del Mar, C.B.E. Weekend courses are four days, from Friday supper to Sunday tea. Price-list from Mr Hearn.

### Law
No restrictions.

### Advertising
You can advertise in professional music magazines and other education outlets. (The Rural Music Schools Association tell me: 'The shortage of good piano teachers is such that he or she is invariably in the position of being overwhelmed with requests from pupils for tuition.')

### What you can earn
Consult the Association. If you live in a rural area and your pupils visit you, your rates will obviously be lower than if you had to bear travel expenses yourself.

### Advantages
This can be pleasing work; especially if you have one or two promising pupils.

### Disadvantages
Endless scales can be tedious.

---

## *Nurse*  M/F  18–55

### *(and Midwife)*

The work described in this section is for part-time nursing outside the home; or for taking part in a 'Nurse Bank' for hospitals; or for nursing patients in your own home; or for occupational health nursing in industry.

No investment. Steady (but not high) income.

### Qualifications
You must first train to become either a State Enrolled or State Registered Nurse.

### Training
One school of nursing in Portsmouth provides part-time courses of approximately three years and two months leading to State Registration.

### How to train
Many schools offer part-time courses leading to State Enrolment; these courses are approximately two years and six months duration. Training for both the Register and the Roll, whether full or part-time, require periods of duty to be undertaken in the evenings, at week-ends and on night duty.

I am told by the Nursing and Health Service Careers Centre: 'Having qualified either as an enrolled or registered nurse, a part-time post may be obtained in either the hospital or community. In addition, many married women have in recent times joined "Nurse Banks"; by this they are able to indicate regularly to their local hospital at what times they may be called upon for temporary nursing duty. Some have also joined nursing agencies on a part-time basis.

'Nursing auxiliaries receive no formal training and gain no recognised certificate; many hospitals do however, have their own "in-service" training. Nursing auxiliaries assist the doctors and nurses in the wards and departments of the hospital and are valuable members of the hospital team. Many married women obtain part-time posts as nursing auxiliaries in both the hospital and the community.'

## Home Nursing

The Royal College of Nursing and National Council of Nurses of the United Kingdom say: 'The Red Cross and St John's Ambulance Brigade run courses in home nursing which are valuable; information concerning these is available from the organisations concerned.

'Up to three elderly persons may be given residential accommodation in a private home, without nursing care being provided beyond the kind of care provided within a family for a relative in the event of a chill, etc., and without the need for special formalities or a nurse being available.'

This is put in another way by the Nursing and Health Service Careers Centre: 'Formal training, experience as a nursing auxiliary or success in a St John's Ambulance or Red Cross Home Nursing Certificate would be invaluable as preparation for nursing your family or friends in their own homes, but only those who are either registered or enrolled may practise as nurses.'

The Centre adds: 'Amongst the other posts offering hours suitable to married women and mothers who have had nursing training are receptionists to either doctors or dentists, phlebotomists who are employed in the clinical laboratories of hospitals to take blood from the veins of patients requiring haematological investigation, occupational health nursing in either industry or educationalist establishments.'

## Equipment

Does not apply.

## Premises

If you should decide to give elderly persons residential accommodation in your own home (with or without trained nursing), you must – if you accommodate more than three persons – register your premises with your local Social Services Department. (See *Host Family (2)* page 45).

As you will have seen from the above remarks, you can use your own spare rooms to nurse elderly patients only if you have trained and qualified as a nurse.

## Write to

The Royal College of Nursing and National Council of Nurses of the United Kingdom, Henrietta Place, Cavendish Square, London W1M 0AB (Tel: 01-580 2646), or to: the Principal Information Officer, Nursing and Health Service Careers Centre, 121/123 Edgware Road, London W2 (Tel: 01-402 5296/7 and/or to: your local Health Department. Also write to: The British Nursing Association, Freepost, 32, London, W1E 3YZ.

## Law

'It is statutory requirement' says the Royal College 'that any premises used or intended to be used for the reception of, and the providing of nursing care for, patients suffering from any sickness, injury or infirmity must be registered as a Nursing Home and any person who carries on a Nursing Home as presently defined, without being registered under the Act, shall be guilty of an offence. (Nursing Homes Act 1975, part 1 (1) and 3 (1).'

## Advertising

'A nurse may use or advertise her professional qualification (1) by nameplate outside her house (2) by letter headings, professional cards etc. (3) in the medical and nursing press (4) by writing to or calling on doctors, hospitals, nursing and old persons' homes, nursing agencies, etc and (5) in lecturing, writing books or on TV but not (in this last case), to advertise herself as a nurse.

'A nurse is not allowed to let her name and nursing qualifications be used for the advertising of any commercial product or service; or to allow her name to appear on the notepaper or other stationery of any person, company or body except that of hospital, nursing or old persons' home, clinic, nursing agency etc.' (Extract from the General Nursing Council for England and Wales Annual Report for 1973–74.)

**What you can earn**
From the Royal College of Nursing (at the above address) you can get a booklet: *The privately employed nurse: Recommended fees and conditions of service.*

This gives full details of hours of duty, meals on duty, pay and tax, travelling expenses or midwifery cases, professional indemnity and so on. However, present N.H.S. salaries based on a 37½ hour week are as follows: State Enrolled Nurse £3,781–£4,561; Staff Nurse £4,198–£5,119; Ward Sister £5,309–£6,807.

## *Odd Jobs*   M/F   12–75

Including 1. Bed-and-breakfast
Newsagent's help and/or theatre programme-person
3. Fish-fingers for schools
4. Cooking-for-markets
5. Pheasant-plucker
6. Whittling
7. Children's library-parlour
8. Pop group impresario
9. Sheepdog knitter

Some irregular income. Any of these odd jobs might develop into rather more than a small, irregular income. All can be done at home or from home.

### 1. Bed-and-breakfast
*Qualifications (including Training, Equipment, Advertising)*

Many people throughout Britain now put a notice in the window offering 'Bed and Breakfast'. You need your own home with window facing the street; your own washing-machine and if possible your own hens in the yard to provide breakfast eggs. You need a spare bedroom and washing facilities.

*Law*
No restriction for b&b but it is safer if you own your own home. If you rent your home, neighbours could make trouble for you.

*What you can earn*
Friends of mine doing this in the West Country usually charge £4.50 per night, £6.50 with evening meal. (All cheaper than most clean good commercial lodgings.) Lowest rate charged was £3.75 a night. I was told that over the past three years, all such guests 'were charming and easy'. We made quite a lot of money and enjoyed doing it.'

### 2. Newsagent's help and/or theatre programme person

*Qualifications, etc.*
You must be an early riser by nature. Good health, a car, bike, scooter or good walking-shoes.

You will discover your nearest newsagent finds it difficult to find and keep reliable delivery-boys or girls.

*What you can earn*
It means roughly three-quarters of an hour's work between 7 a.m. and 7.45

a.m. for a six day week to earn between £3 and £4.50 per week depending on the distance you cover.

However, you could make more money by doing an evening shift in your local theatre as freelance programme-seller. You'll find you are not expected to stay long after the curtain goes up.

### 3. Fish-fingers for schools

*Qualifications, etc.*
I use this only as my title: Fish-fingers for schools can cover a variety of activities.

A good husband-and-wife job which is often advertised in provincial evening papers is, for example, to work on a motorised caravan after permission has been granted by the Local Authority for the caravan to do business in car parks or near schools or colleges. The only snag is you are expected to put down a lump sum of £150 on the caravan (which remains the property of the employers); you buy all food from them, e.g. hamburgers, fish fingers, pies, etc., and any profit on top of that is yours. It would be a better commercial proposition if you had your own caravan, from which you could sell hot chips, fish fingers, etc., but in this case you yourself must approach the Local Authority for permission. Now that schoolchildren's lunches are a problem you will find a more sympathetic ear to your request for a licence.

*What you can earn*
This could be a big earner if (a) you can get permission and (b) you can also satisfy the local Fire Service that you know what you are doing.

(I do know of several village bakers, one in Surrey and one in Sussex, who run a kind of informal fish-and-chip shop in the shed at the bottom of their gardens for two evenings a week. In between they bake bread, doughnuts and lardy cake and deliver it themselves to the one village shop.)

### 4. Cooking-for-markets

*Qualifications, etc.*
This is similar work to the above and the same conditions apply. (Unless you are a member of the W.I., supplying cooked food to one of their regular weekly markets, in which case you need no one's permission.)

But try extending this by baking scones, cakes, etc., loading them into your car and driving to the nearest open market and sell them to stalls or hire your own stall (price of a provincial market stall can range from £5 to £7 for a period from 8 a.m. Saturday, say, to 1 p.m.)

### 5. Pheasant-plucker

*Qualifications, etc.*
Poulterers are finding it more and more difficult to find pluckers with the skill to pluck pheasants, fowl, geese, turkeys, etc., ready for the table. Apply to local farms, poulterers, and offer to do the feather-plucking at home if you live nearby.

This is work most available before Easter and Christmas holidays. Earnings are small, but you may get the chance of a cheap Christmas turkey on top.

### 6. Whittling

*Qualifications, etc.*
You need a talent for drawing/art. I know men and women who make marvellous animals out of wood, by whittling away with a pen-knife. I am told 'an odd-shaped piece of wood can remind you of something, i.e. a tiger's face, so you carve it into a tiger, or a leaping salmon, or a bear'. Then you polish them (or paint them) until the animals look quite professional. (I have heard of people making these figures out of soap.)

*What you can earn*
These wooden animals whittled from a piece of wood, sell for quite a lot of money in gift-shops, etc.

### 7. Children's library-parlour

*Qualifications, etc.*
This is a new idea described in a recent radio programme by a woman who organised a Children's Library in her front parlour. This was in a large village which had no public library and no shops. Although the county library service called regularly to stand for some hours in the village street where people could change their library books, there were no facilities for children. This lady already had a large number of children's books and stories left over from her own family, so she bought more paperbacks for young children and set up a library in her front window. She charged a few pennies only for each book and a small fine for delay in return. Her library was a small earner but it became a children's centre for social activities, tea, etc.

### 8. Pop group impresario

*Qualifications, etc.*
The time has gone when you could form your own group and find yourselves in the Top Ten almost overnight. However, if you are interested in pop music, and if you know some young people who could form a musical group with a soloist who has his or her own special style this is a good way of starting your own business in the style of The Good Companions, except that you need no premises and can practise in your own homes. What you need as impresario for your own group is a small capital with which to finance the first steps, such as advertising, correspondence, research and travel costs to organise the first auditions for your group. Try and get as much free help as possible from your local Radio, local Press and Local Authority. You could start doing this by offering to entertain free for a charitable cause.

*What you can earn*
Most of the rich and powerful groups in the world today, began in this way, with nothing but a belief in their own enterprise and talent. But you do need a name.

There is no reason why such groups should always be young; it would be a splendid gimmick to start the first middle-aged one!

### 9. Sheepdog knitter

*Qualifications, etc.*
If you are interested in crafts such as weaving and spinning which you can learn by joining the W.I., or by taking one of many craft courses mentioned in *Craft Worker*, page 24 and/or *Leather Worker*, page 54, you will be interested in certain people in the Home Counties who keep Old English sheepdogs. They cut, weave and they knit the dogs' hairs into attractive sweaters.

*What you can earn*
The sweaters fetch good prices in local shops, boutiques or when exhibited in the nearest pub!

---

## Patchwork quilt maker   M/F   16–90

Very low investment. Fair to modest income. Can be done at home.

**Qualifications**
Sewing and designing ability. Taste in colour and shape. Patience.

**Equipment**
There is now a new, simple way of doing the hexagons, half hexagons and triangles. It is a new product called Patchwork Papers, which are a pack of 25 sheets of press-out, cut patchwork

67

shapes, hexagons, diamonds, half hexagons and triangles. New packs in varying shapes are being made for 1981.

**Write to**
Hilary Warren, Patchwork Papers, 14 Dundonald Close, Hayling Island, at around £3 per pack, post and packing inclusive.

Also ask all your friends to let you have all their left-over bits of material.

Look in *Vogue* magazine or *The Lady* where you will see advertisements from time to time of offers of patchwork pieces as well as in other magazine pattern books sections.

Also try Laura Ashley, who supply bags of sprigged cotton prints for 50p to £1 a bag. Few firms sell these bags of fabric pieces so it is worth writing to Laura Ashley to ask how you could get hold of them, as she only supplied them to personal shoppers at 40 Sloane Street, London, SW1.

Helpful books include: *The Seven-day Quilt* by Josephine Rogers (a paperback published Mills and Boon, £3.95) instructs you how to make a quilt in 7 days! Also *The McCall Book of Quilts* published John Murray, £5.95. Both are good books for beginners.

**Advertising**
In your local paper, magazine or newsagent. I quote a recent advertisement from a Hastings newspaper; 'a patchwork quilt, hand sewn, in a glory of warm browns, creams and russet pinks, softly padded £98.'

**What you can earn**
If you work at the rate of about three hours a day, it might take you as long as three months to complete a quilt. Current prices being charged are between £95 and £125 per quilt. You can sell them at a W.I. market (they charge you a small commission for this), or you can also hawk them round fairly ritzy shops or advertise in magazines like *The Lady*.

**Advantages**
If it's one way of getting you to join the W.I., then it's worth it. It helps to belong to a 'club' like that. And, personally, I adore the W.I. – which is, of course, the National Federation of Women's Institutes (see *Useful Contacts*).

**Disadvantages**
Family and friends tend to walk off with your bits of patchwork – just because they fancy the colours!

---

## *Photographer*   M/F   22–60

---

Fairly high investment. Very good income. Can be done at home or from home.

**Qualifications**
It depends what kind of photography you want to do. If you want to work mostly at home and not travel further than your local wedding, flower show or office party, then there is nothing to stop you working purely as an amateur, self-taught, without belonging to any trade union or professional body. (I am told by photographers with whom I have worked many years in newspapers that there is a living to be

made simply by concentrating on local weddings, or doing portrait photography of local families or birthdays.)

However, if you want to work in journalism or to do any kind of specialist photography such as medical or scientific work, then you must join the I.I.P. (see below) or the N.U.J. (National Union of Journalists) or other relevant organisation or institute.

For instance, if a railway or aircraft accident took place near your home and you had the chance to be first on the scene to take a photograph and sell it to a newspaper, you might possibly be prevented by the police or other authority unless you could show your credentials. If an amateur took such a picture, and if it were good enough, any newspaper would buy it (probably paying less than the normal fee required by an N.U.J. man or woman); but the chances are that the police would not allow him to approach, simply because of his amateur status.

## Training
Specialist training: You must be at least 21, and have had three years experience as a photographer. You can apply to the Chief Executive of the I.I.P. (Institute of Incorporated Photographers) – a qualifying organisation, with a responsibility for photographic education. It provides technical advice for members and represents the profession.

To work in newspapers, see under *Journalist* (page 48). There are various degrees of membership of the I.I.P. Entrance fees and annual subscriptions include Corporate Membership £38 per annum, Graduate Membership £10 and Affiliate Membership £25 per annum. You can also get a list of schools from the I.I.P.

## Equipment
You will need camera, lenses, enlargers, and all the processing equipment for your studio and dark room for developing your pictures.

## Premises
A specially-equipped studio at home.

## Write to
The Secretary, Institute of Incorporated Photographers, Amwell End, Ware, Herts. SG12 9HN (Tel: Ware 4011).

## Law
The Institute lays down a code of conduct you must obey as a member.

There is also a code of safety covering general principles, your legal responsibility, and fire precautions.

The Institute has a list of books containing all the necessary instructions on the laws of photography; these cover such things as photographic models, copyright, and colour pictures.

## Advertising
Rules about this are included in the I.I.P's code of conduct.

## What you can earn
If you join the I.I.P., you have to keep to a scale charge. But if you remain freelance, you can fix your own charges for weddings, portraits etc. You can earn good money.

## Advantages
I think the money; also it's interesting work and could be fairly regular, provided your home is not surrounded by too much local competition. So enquire first in your district.

## Disadvantages
I worked with press photographers for many, many years and found many of them to be somewhat neurotic. They were Big Worriers. I can't really explain why.

---

## *Pippa-Dee party giver*    18–35

Fairly small investment. Good income. Can be done from home.

## Qualifications and training
No training or special qualifications required except for three hours training in your own home by a manager.

The manager will then help you with your first few parties, while you grow in confidence.

Pippa-Dee issue you with a range of

garments, lingerie, underwear and outerwear, free; you attend fortnightly meetings to keep you abreast of developments, and once a month the range is updated. Clothes which are withdrawn from their selection become your own. The outerwear (slacks, skirts etc.) carry a six-month normal-wear guarantee.

### What you can earn

Pippa-Dee Parties, whose idea this is, tell me that 'this could net you about £15 to £17 for two parties or five hours' work a week. The orders are delivered to the party's hostess and she has to collect payment. You are simply the organiser of the party and you do not handle either the goods or the money.

'For this the party-giver gets the Pippa-Dee products to the value of 12½% on orders taken in her home, while you as organiser get a commission which can rise to 20%.'

The company also has a children's-wear department called Dee Minor for which the same scheme operates.

### Write to

The Sales Director, Pippa-Dee Parties Ltd, Anglesey House, Anglesey Road, Burton-on-Trent DE14 3QD. (Tel: Burton-on-Trent 66344).

### Advantages

According to women who have tried it, they enjoy the parties anyway!

The garments you are selling are of comparable quality to those sold in the shops, and so you will probably find it easy to gain custom.

It's a good way of meeting people.

### Disadvantages

Unless you are a genuinely sociable person, and interested in clothes, you may find the parties tiresome after a while. Also it tends to be very much a woman's world, which might not be your ideal.

---

## *Potter*  M/F  9–65

---

Investment can amount to several hundred pounds or more for good electrical equipment. However it can be done for much less by buying secondhand, but life of secondhand equipment will be shorter. Income is steady, fairly good and modestly rewarding. Can be done at home, in a studio.

### Qualifications

I am going to quote the opinions of a well known potter in Surrey, who has also run a pottery school, and taught both adults and children to be potters on weekday and holiday courses. Peter S. E. Thompson and Pamela Thompson of Adsum Cottage Pottery, Hurst Green, Oxted, Surrey RH8 9DU (Tel: Oxted 3608) say: 'Someone without any formal qualifications can become a potter, learning by practice and experience, discussions with other potters, and the use of reference books. There are also L.E.A. classes for adults (both day and evening) in many areas where basic pottery and more advanced work can be learned.'

### Training

'Weekly residential courses are available in parts of the country. These have a big advantage over the two hours per week evening class in that students can participate in the whole process of making a pot – seeing it dry through various stages, decorating it, seeing its first (biscuit) firing and final (glaze) firing.

'Potteries like this advertise their course in papers such as *The Times Educational Supplement* and the *Ceramic Review*. Also see course mentioned in *Leather Worker* page 54 and *Craft Worker* page 24.

## How to train

There are also Diplomas in Ceramics to be gained by study, either full- or part-time, at Technical College such as the North Staffordshire College of Art, Stoke-on-Trent or the John Cass College (London University).

Another approach is to be an apprentice or helper in a large pottery firm or to an established potter; over a number of years this would give invaluable experience. Mr Thompson says that potters arrive at their skill by many different routes; some turn into brilliant teachers, and some who do excellent work may fail if they do not also have the necessary business sense. Some potters work together, often having four different types of kiln in action.

As an example, his week-day course lasts for six weeks, i.e. a total of twelve hours, and the charge is £9. Courses in other parts of the country seem to range from about £20 onwards, excluding accommodation. At Adsum Cottage Pottery, Holiday Courses for children of 9–13 years old take place in the Easter and summer holidays, and the course costs £4 for a total of five hours in each, and includes some of their finished pots. (All prices here are exclusive of V.A.T. and carriage.)

## Equipment

New kilns vary between £80 for a small electric to many hundreds for a large electric kiln, but you might be lucky and get a secondhand one for much less. Mr Thompson says that you can make your own kiln for half that price. Electric kilns, he says, are the best for predictable results and although the cost in electricity is high, the price of electricity per ounce of pot is a matter of a few pence. Other kilns . . . gas, oil, wood can be made to produce interesting results but cost, installation and local bylaws can be serious problems.

Kick wheels cost between £125 and £380.

Podmores of Stoke-on-Trent make a kit of the essential mechanical parts of a simple kick wheel for about £70. They also produce a geared kick wheel which can reach motor speeds of 300 revolutions per minute.

Electric wheels cost £200 to £500. Podmores of Stoke-on-Trent have a good range, and so do Wengers of Stoke-on-Trent.

Mr Thompson also recommends a pug-mill which mixes and squeezes clay for re-use and is very useful. The present price is about £415 for a motorised one.

However, secondhand equipment often comes on to the market. Study the *Ceramic Review* for these bargains. A good knowledge of prices and equipment is really necessary if secondhand equipment is considered. The newest development is probably the introduction of ceramic fibre, which can stand up to very high temperatures in the kiln, enabling a 50% reduction in units of electricity used (see *Useful Contacts* for supplier).

## Premises

A studio in your home; or you can make one out of a garden shed or your garage, but access to electricity and water is essential.

## Write to

Your Local Adult Education Centre (the Principal); your local Arts Guild or Association or to one of the Federation of British Craft Societies (see *Useful Contacts*).

## Law

It is advisable to inform your Local Authority, or to consult C.A.B. to find out the procedure in your area, if fuel other than electricity is to be used. Some Councils will make no demands or think of restricting you in any way; others will want to know that you are keeping within the byelaws.

## Advertising

Again I quote Mr Thompson: 'Having decided to become a potter, over a period of about two years I subdivided my time between making and selling pottery, running classes at my home and teaching for Surrey County Council in Adult Education Centres. Since then the demand for adult and especially children's courses has grown considerably.

'I advertised in local shops, some twelve in all. Just a simple card with POTTERY COURSES in bold letters, my name and telephone number. This method produced most of my students. The local papers also advertised my courses on occasions. Local organisations such as the Women's Institutes, art societies and churches were also informed. After this word of mouth, and the same students coming again and again, has yielded sufficient pupils. Children's courses fill up quickly and should be booked well in advance.'

Private orders often develop from small displays at home or at an exhibition. Ask your local arts society or guild if you can participate in any of their exhibitions. (Mr Thompson actually put some of his pots on show in the windows of Building Societies; they were probably pleased with the decoration as it helped them, too, to attract customers!)

**What you can earn**
You must fix your own prices by costing your time and materials, and looking at what other potters charge. Among the easiest lines to sell are bowls of different sizes, vases, jugs, mugs and candle-sticks, (and animals and figures such as hedgehogs, owls and pigs).

**Advantages**
This is creative work that appears to create happiness for all concerned with it. I have met a lot of potters (as well as the dedicated Mr Thompson) and they are all contented, if not outstandingly rich.

**Disadvantages**
Investment, as you can see from the above, is not all that cheap. You may need a loan from the bank, or else you'll have to save up hard. COSIRA may be able to get you a loan by putting in a good word for you at the bank, if you can give employment to other persons. (See *Useful Contacts* for address of COSIRA, in Scotland and Wales also.)

Go to evening classes first to make sure you have the talent.

---

## Pre-school playgroup organiser   M/F   18–45

---

No investment (almost). Very little income. Can be done in your own home, someone else's, in a local hall or large room.

**Qualifications**
It is not necessary to be trained, though a short course is helpful (see below). But certain criteria must be met regarding premises and number of children

**Training**
You can attend various courses of training in your own area. These sometimes take the form of a short series of evening talks and sometimes a year-long course on one day a week. Although these courses do not, so far, provide you with a degree or diploma they are valuable training for those people working in playgroups and for mothers generally.

**How to train**
Few details of the various courses you can attend you should contact your nearest Voluntary Area Organiser of the Pre-School Playgroups Association, Alford House, Aveline Street, London SE11 5DH. (Tel: 01-582 8871).

For details of a Pre-School Play Group Certificate Course you should contact the Principal of Chelmsford College of Further Education (Essex County Council) at Upper Moulsham Street, Chelmsford, CM2 0QJ (Tel: Chelmsford 65611 Ext. 32/22) and ask whether this course is available in your particular local area. At Chelmsford this course is held on one day per week from 10.00 a.m. to 3.00 p.m. There is also a Pre-School Play Group Centre on the College campus and student mothers can arrange for their younger children to attend while they are in formal classes.

## Equipment

Playgroup equipment, including the instructions for how to make it. Playgroup woodwork, music, badges, balloons and exhibition kit.

Investment is mainly in playgroup membership fees as follows: subscription is £10 per year, of which £4.80 goes to the National Association and £1.20 to the member's branch, County Association and region. (This provides 10 issues of *Contact* the playgroup magazine every year, quarterly copies of *Under 5*, the parents' magazine; an insurance scheme, one vote at national and local levels; catalogues, special offers etc., from suppliers of toys and equipment; P.P.A. publications at discount price; an introduction to an area organiser; specialist advice and support; a copy of P.P.A's annual report.)

Or you can buy individual membership: for this the subscription is £10 per year (£5 per half year) and is available to (a) persons not directly concerned with running playgroups; (b) persons associated with playgroups that have playgroup membership. For this you get 10 issues of *Contact* per year; a quarterly copy of *Under 5*, one vote at national and local levels; P.P.A. publications at discount price, a copy of the annual report.

## Premises

It is always a problem to find suitable premises. The nearest available church hall or schoolroom is the most suitable, especially if it has a garden or open space attached and there must be lavatory accommodation suitable for toddlers. Ideally there should be at least one teacher-in-charge but as many mothers as possible to act as volunteer 'teachers'.

## Write to

The Pre-School Playgroups Association.

## Advertising

Any advertising will take place within P.P.A. journals like *Contact* etc. But local contacts soon build up.

## What you can earn

The Secretary of the P.P.A. says that playgroup work is not usually very well paid. The majority of play leaders work on a part-time basis, sometimes employed by a voluntary parent committee. The modest pay varies considerably from one district to another, because there is no standard rate but is dependent on hours worked and conditions.

## Advantages

It's one of the few jobs where you can take your children with you! If you have young children, you'll not only enjoy it but you'll make good friends in your neighbourhood. If you have an only child, that child will soon have some good friends too.

## Disadvantages

Don't go near this job, unless you sincerely like and enjoy children.

## Note

For details of teacher training or nursery-nurse courses in your area, you should enquire at your local Education Office.

Medium to very high investment (depending on whether you want to make 'pin-money' or a commercial success). High income for a commercial venture only. Can be done at home.

### Qualifications and training
Some experience of keeping rabbits is essential if you do this on any scale. Your market for grown rabbits must also be assured. The Commercial Rabbit Association recommend that a beginner should start with only a few breeding does to gain experience in handling and care. To rear rabbits – even just a few – demands knowledge in the basic care of animals, so start with a 'pilot' unit of less than 50 does as this will enable you, a novice, to develop some sort of affinity with the rabbit.

The Association provides educational courses and also day-conferences in various parts of the country. There are lectures, practical instruction and farm visits with ample time for questions and discussion. Any age group is welcome to attend the courses (there have been students as young as 12, and the upper age group has no limit); many retired people attend the courses, which are held in different places around the country. Enquiries to the Association

### How to train
The Association say: 'Sufficient capital will be required to carry the farm for two years. Whether the unit be a part-time venture or a 200–400 doe, one-man unit, it is the management and attention to detail by the individual running the unit which is of over-riding importance.'

### Equipment
A rabbit might cost from £4.50 to £8 at twelve weeks. It needs a cage of 10 sq. ft., which must be dry, draught-free and vermin-proof, with artificial or natural light. Also feed hoppers, drinkers and nest boxes.

### Premises
A small garden or backyard is suitable only for very small-scale investors; rabbit farming on a commercial level demands considerable housing and unless you already have suitable out-buildings for both the rabbits and food storage, with mains, water and electricity, it would be very expensive to set up.

### Write to
The Secretary of the Commercial Rabbit Association, Tyning House, Shurdington, Cheltenham, Gloucester GL51 5XF (Tel: Cheltenham 862 387. (Membership £8 per annum).

### Law
You are advised to inform the local Council if you keep more than a few but the Commercial Rabbit Association will be glad to advise you, even if you don't want to become a member.

### Advertising
No restrictions, but ask the Council first.

### What you can earn
The Commercial Rabbit Association say: 'Profitability is related to the effort and expertise of the individual concerned etc.'

### Advantages
Each female rabbit is capable of producing at least 15 times her own weight in meat rabbits per year. We've all been warned that meat will get scarcer and dearer, so the role of the rabbit seems secure for the future.

### Disadvantages
Despite what the Commercial Rabbit Association call the rabbit's prolificacy,

you clearly need to invest quite a bit of money to make it commercial. And, as with any animals you keep, you are tied down.

## *Researcher and social survey interviewer* M/F 20–45

### Researcher
This job can sometimes be seen being done by young women standing among the shopping crowds in any High Street, holding a questionnaire and pen. From time to time they approach at random one of the shoppers to ask what kind of biscuit is preferred, what radio programmes liked, or what are the family habits regarding dental drill or holidays. The researchers are employed by a variety of manufacturers, advertisers, organisations, charities, universities and by the B.B.C. and less frequently by I.T.V. who sometimes use their own staff for research.

### Social survey interview
The job of social survey interviewer is done for the purpose of population censuses and surveys, which is of course more serious, important and requires total accuracy.

No investment. Can be done from home in your local area but only in an urban or suburban environment. Modest to small income.

### Qualifications and training
Clear handwriting.

For market research: An interview followed by some training in the office and some outside work under supervision.

For B.B.C. and occasionally for I.T.V. research: you must be free for training and for work two weeks in a row. Two hours a day but seven days a week when in progress.

For social survey interviewing: a good educational background.

### Equipment
Telephone (but not essential). Car for

television and radio research is useful. Television set and radio set and/or transistor.

### Premises
You can work from home but there is obviously a certain amount of local travelling and visiting.

### Write to
The Secretary, The Market Research Society, 15 Belgrade Square, London SW1X 8PF (Tel: 01-235 4709), and ask them to send you their booklet of all the firms in the Society who employ home-workers.

Also to the B.B.C. Fieldwork Organiser, Audience Research Department, B.B.C. London W1A 1AA, and to your local B.B.C. and I.T.V. offices in such places as Manchester, Liverpool, Glasgow, Cardiff etc.

Social survey interviewer applicants should write to the Office of Population Censuses and Surveys (Social Science Division), St Catherine's House, 10 Kingsway, London WC2B 6JP (Tel: 01-242 0262 Extension 2307).

### *Training for social survey interviewing*
Recruits are selected by interviews held in provincial offices throughout the country (held in rooms loaned for the purpose).

### How to train
This important work requires absolute accuracy of fieldwork. So those applicants short-listed to attend for a personal interview are also asked to take a simple test to assess clerical accuracy and the ability to follow and apply instructions. Interviewers must be trained in specific methods of

interviewing and those people who are successful at the recruitment interview are invited to London for a 3-day training session for discussion and practise.

Interviewers must be willing and able to work at least 3 days to include a minimum of 3 evenings per week (approximately 24–28 hours per week for part-time work), but can work any number above up to 5 or 6 days and 4 or 5 evenings for full time work. Work on a survey usually lasts 4 to 6 weeks though this can vary. On the application form you should state the amount of time you want to work. Hours may be very irreguluar – say up to 10.00 p.m. or in the early morning to fit in with the hours of people to be interviewed.

Regular work cannot be guaranteed, so those people able to travel further and work longer will get the available work.

You have to supply personal references, from past or present employers.

## Equipment
Obviously a car or other transport.

## Premises
There is a certain amount of homework attached to each survey and this, of course, is the only part of the work you can do in your own home.

## Law
The information given on all surveys is treated as strictly confidential; no names are given in survey reports, and interviewers must never divulge the names of anyone they have on their list for interview.

## Advertising
Is not allowed.

## What you can earn
As a researcher pay is modest.

As a social survey interviewer rates of pay vary; in addition, you get subsistence and expenses. Hourly rate: trainee £2.09; trained £2.34; Merit 1 £2.42; Merit 2 £2.50; Merit 3 £2.68. London weighting, for those living within five miles of Charing Cross 62p per hour; for those living 5 to 18 miles of Charing Cross 26p per hour. Subsistence allowance (for staying away from home overnight): Inner London £27; Outer London £21.20. Day subsistence for over 5 hours up to 10 hours £1.50; over 10 hours £3.55. Cars: 16.2p to 19.1p per mile. Public transport: 9.6p per mile.

## Advantages
Interesting work sometimes.

## Disadvantages
You may be out in all weathers. Most vacancies tend to be in or near big towns in England and Scotland, or sometimes South Wales.

---

## *Room-letter*  M/F  21–80

---

Some investment needed. (But you might get a grant.) Small regular income. Can be done at home.

## Qualifications
You must have one or more rooms to let in your own flat or house. You must have permission from your landlord or Local Council if the property is not your own.

## Training
None needed. But commonsense and discipline essential. (e.g. if you are a woman living alone, do not let a room to a man who is a complete stranger without references.)

## How to train
By experience. Write to Mr C. R. Stringer, Director, Finance and Ad-

ministration, British Property Federation, 35 Catherine Place, London SW1E 6DY (Tel: 01-828 0111). I suggest you join this body for your own protection. It is non-party and non-profit making. It is, in effect, the successor to the National Association of Property Owners. The B.P.F. give an advisory service to members on law, management and administration of property and on taxation, housing and rating problems; supports certain approved test cases in the courts and keeps you informed on current government measures and laws. It costs only between £7 and £20 a year. I say 'only' because of what I've learned about the problems of landladies and landlords.

It seems that anyone letting rooms needs all the advice, support and protection they can get. Among other warnings, Mr R. H. Shrives, the Secretary of the Brighton, Hove and District Landlords and Property Owners Association, 77 Peacock Lane, Brighton BN1 6WA (Tel: Brighton (0273) 554312) said that prospective landlords (resident) would be well advised to consult an accountant before letting, to obtain some idea of their possible liability.

They should also be made aware of the difficult, perhaps impossible, situation which will arise if a resident landlord dies when a tenant is in occupation. The Rent Act of 1974 gives a resident landlord a right of possession for tenancies granted after the date when the Act became operative, 14 August 1974, although this is a right which can only be exercised after a long and expensive process of litigation.

Mr Shrives added: 'In my opinion, the only safe thing for a resident landlord to do is to let on a bed-and-breakfast basis, because this will not create a tenancy, and the occupant can be required to go at any time.'

*Important:* Mr Shrives went to a great deal of trouble to make me aware of all the risks involved and I have a responsibility to my readers. So let me put in his most urgent remark: 'Those who still decide to let should not allow a tenant to take up occupation until a tenancy agreement has been signed by both parties and stamped by the Inland Revenue. The agreement should for safety be drawn up by a solicitor, and should incorporate an inventory of furniture provided, and a schedule of conditions, prepared by a professional man. This will be expensive, perhaps £20 to £40 but may save trouble later on.' Mr Stringer of the B.P.F. says a leaflet of advice can be obtained from Catherine Place (see above) for a small fee.

## Equipment

You might be able to get a grant from your Local Authority to improve the accommodation to enable you to let the rooms: e.g. to install wash-basin, additional piped water supply, equipment for gas-ring or cooking-stove etc.

If you live in or near a University town and want to let rooms to students (there is a big demand) then you need no other equipment than that mentioned above, i.e. wash-basin, water supply, gas-ring or cooking-stove. Students prefer to 'do' for themselves entirely, making their own beds, cleaning their own rooms and providing their own sheets, towels, linen etc.

With other lodgers who require part or full-service, you must have extra supplies of sheets, towels, blankets and so on. (You will be able to claim against tax for their use.)

## Premises

Any extra space you have can be let to someone. In the case of students, an official from the University is likely to call to inspect the accommodation in the first instance.

## Write to

The Warden or Accommodation Office at the University and ask for your name to be put on the list of Students' Accommodation. Also to the British Property Federation (see *How to Train* above). Also write to: Mrs L. Cline,

Secretary, Small Landlords Association, 7 Rosedene Avenue, Streatham, London, SW16 (Tel: 01-769 5060). Send for her publication *Letters from Landlords* costing about £2.50 or £3. Enclose self-addressed and stamped envelope.

## Law

If you live in a council house, ask the Housing Officer or your local Council whether sub-letting is permitted.

If you decide to make large structural alterations to your own property in order to have a self-contained flat or flatlet, write first to the Planning Officer's Department at your Council Headquarters. If you want it so self-contained that the flatlet has its own front door, this may alter the appearance of your house or apartments. (The Planning Authorities might not approve this.)

Ask either the C.A.B. or your Council offices whether it is necessary for you to register your accommodation. Don't forget that if you let rooms, you'll be liable for capital gains tax when you sell your home.

## Advertising

Put a brief, informative advertisement in your local newspaper, giving details of what you have to offer. Use a box number or telephone number rather than your address.

## What you can earn

This is up to you. However, for students there is a more or less fixed rate. A bedsitter, self-contained with no food or service, used to be depending on the size of the room, £6 or £7, or even more in London for a 'superior' room. Nowadays the rate is about £13 per week inclusive of electricity and gas. You do better if you do meals for them. A friend of mine in Manchester charges her two students about £28 each with all meals included. There is something called a 'University Agreement' and their Accommodation Office will advise you if you telephone. Several students in the one house are happy to share their own 'kitchen' or cooking facilities or gas-ring etc. They provide their own china etc. However, nowadays some landlords provide bed-and-breakfast for non-students as a safeguard – and a box of cornflakes won't do!

## Advantages

You are entirely free, especially with students who need nothing in the way of cleaning and cooking.

## Disadvantages

You have lost your total privacy. You can't run about the house half-naked as you used to do for instance! But most important is that of the possible difficulty of getting rid of tenants.

## Comments

State your rules at the outset. Be firm. Insist on no late coming home at night. No noisy radios. Permit girl or boy friends, however, if that suits you. Students require their own key to your front door. And do choose whom you let to with care.

---

## *Servicemaster's assistant*   M/F   20–45

The Servicemaster kind of service was originally an American idea and every town in the U.S.A. has either an office or local representative. It spread to Britain many years ago and most big towns have a local representative. The work is nearly always done by men who have to be trained and skilled in furniture-removal, the use of cleaning tools and all domestic cleaning methods. Formerly used mostly by stately homes and the houses of busy, wealthy people, the service in the last few decades has spread to ordinary homes, council housing estates and is specially helpful to working housewives who have no time for the traditional 'spring-clean'.

No investment needed. Good income but intermittent. Can be done near your own home, in your own neighbourhood. It includes: delivering curtains or carpets (by van or car); crockery-washing; ornament and brass cleaning; paintwork and general cleaning; telephone sitting or answering; leaflet delivering; typing; driving etc. All this work would be to *help and assist the Servicemaster operator* himself in his and your local area.

### Qualifications
The usual housewifery ones.

### Training
No training is needed, provided you have normal skill and ability in handling china and ornaments and understand the normal housewife's use of detergents and cleaning materials.

### Equipment
Any equipment you possess will come in handy: a car, typewriter, telephone, brushes, pans, cleaning utensils.

### Premises
Some of the jobs done for Servicemaster could be collected (if you have a car or van) and taken home to be done and then delivered later.

### Write to
Servicemaster Ltd, 50 Commercial Square, Freeman's Common, Leicester LE2 7SR (Tel: Leicester (0533); 548620).

This is a widespread organisation with branches and representatives in most cities of Britain. (I discovered it when I once employed a Servicemaster representative for a day in my flat and wrote about the experience in the *Daily Telegraph*.)

The firm's Director, Mr. B. A. Smith says: 'Some of our single associates look for house-bound ladies who are willing to offer a telephone answering service. Other associates are using ladies to deliver promotional material or canvass. Some may use a secretarial service which could be a person on their own. Occasionally, where we are involved in disaster restoration work after fire or flood, we have passed out cleaning work of books and/or children's toys.'

### Law
No restrictions. (But don't forget to ask for equal pay with men.)

### What you can earn
The only point in offering to do these jobs would be the money. However, the local representative told me: 'I cannot quote the terms as there are no fixed rates. It depends upon the individual and their experience.'

### Advantages
It should be interesting work. The firm claims to work for the very rich, doing removals and cleaning the more stately kind of homes.

### Disadvantages
Flood and fire disasters don't happen, fortunately, every day, and you don't want to hang about!

---

## *Teas and refreshments*   M/F   18–50

---

Fairly high investment needed. Fairly high income can be expected (if your home is in an attractive spot).

Can be done at home.

### Qualifications
This is perhaps the only job in the book where your home and garden and their qualifications are more important than

yours. Even if your home is fairly hard to find and difficult to reach . . . it should not affect your success too much. People in motorcars are looking for the quiet, out-of-the-way-spots to get away-from-it-all and since the war thousands of 'Teas' cafes throughout Britain have closed down. Every week-end, especially Sunday, millions of motoring families go out looking for the handful which are still open. This despite tea flasks and caravans! What families are seeking is old-style country tea, including fresh scones, cream and jam, large piping hot tea made in earthenware tea-pots, china cups not plastic ones. (There are plenty of can-teens and motorway cafeterias with all-plastic crockery and all-plastic food.)

What you need is a downstairs room in your house large enough to take a few tea-tables (for 4), an extra wash-room and lavatory inside or outside the house and a patch of garden or lawn, preferably in front of the house.

### How to train
If you are a good pastry-cook, it helps. Training is mostly by experience and trial and error.

### Equipment and premises
Try the big stores for garden furniture. Buy some made of mixed plastic-and-iron which you can safely leave out in the rain. Also buy some attractive wooden seats and benches. (Look for bargain lots being sold off at sales.) Also buy a double quantity of small trays to hold tea-pots, plates and cutlery, ash-trays (you could make these yourself or get some for almost nothing at jumble sales). Buy far more china crockery than you think you'll need because a lot will be broken by customers and by you or your helpers on busy Sundays.

You will also need: sacks of flour (for scones) if you are doing your own bak-ing; butter, variety of jams, sugar, tea, etc. It is advisable to have a large freezer so that you can freeze any left-overs for another week. Also for keeping cream to be whipped for your cream teas. (Note: do study hygiene laws first.) Also tea-towels and kitchen supplies, detergents etc. Try to make an arrangement with a discount house prepared to deliver to your door for bulk orders (keep a blackboard notice on the kitchen wall where you can chalk up the quantities and dates to remind yourself). Also towels, soap, toilet-rolls, floor mats. Buy strips of cheap motorcar carpeting to protect your hall and living-room in bad weather. This business will be very hard on your carpets. Say £400 worth of goods to launch you in business if you are clever at buying up job lots and sales bargains; otherwise you must spend between £500 and £1,000.

### Write to
Your local Council because you will need permission from their Planning Department and from their Environ-mental Officer, who will check your premises and your kitchen (under the Food Hygiene (1970) regulations). You are strongly advised to buy a copy of the regulations and study them – they cost 10p from H.M.S.O. (see *Useful Contacts*) or through any bookseller. The regulations number is S.I. 1970 No. 1172.

### Law
See remarks above under 'Write to'. The regulations oblige you to provide on your premises water supply, sanit-ary conveniences, washing facilities, first-aid kit, waste disposal, coverings for food and equipment to avoid con-tamination of food.

### Advertise
Advertise in the local and national press, in magazines like *Country Life*, *Tatler* and in gardening and nature journals; also the usual newsagent's card. If you have transport available, have some cards printed and distribute them in your neighbourhood through letter-boxes. If you are, or believe

yourself to be, the only teas/refreshments business in a radius of say 30 miles (which is most likely anyway in south-east England) ring your local evening paper and ask them to do a story on your establishment. (Don't forget to provide a drink for the reporter and photographer when they call.)

*Note:* Even if you are not in a recognised 'beauty spot', even if you live on a great, wind-swept housing estate, 'Teas' etc. is a good money-making idea. Commercial cafes tend to close just when you need them most, i.e. 5 p.m.! If you live near a *school*, open your house to 'Teas' where mothers can wait.

### What you can earn
This is a business where you will need (and I do sincerely recommend it!) the services of an accountant to guide you, because within a few years you may well find yourself in the V.A.T. area. (See Ann's story, earlier in this book.) He may advise you to become licensed to sell sweets, cigarettes and soft drinks also if you are in a fairly remote area. He will also advise you on tax and help you to claim against it. For example, if you are doing the 'serving' of teas as well as the making you are entitled to some relief for your clothing and general appearance in public, as this is part of your working equipment.

### Advantages
Because motoring is now the national pastime, this need no longer be just a seasonal trade but an all-year-round one. On wet days, if you have food left over, you can always eat it yourself or refreeze it (if you are careful about refreezing rules regarding cream etc.). If you live out in the country, you won't be lonely.

### Disadvantages
You might prefer to be lonely! I visited one attractive 'Teas' place (the only one for miles around) in a splendid forest and found it had become so popular with coach parties that it was no longer the peaceful spot 'as advertised'.

## *Telephone salesperson* M/F 25–55

No investment. Fairly modest income – unless you have a 'breakthrough.' Can be done at home.

### Qualifications
Initial selection is made from those with previous selling experience in retailing or media, or from occupations involving wide contact with the public, e.g. market research interviewers, nurses, teachers.

### Training
Having had at some time in your career some sort of market or sales research experience, order collecting and telephone selling experience or experience in fixing appointments. Written instructions are often supported by personal training, also with particular briefing and/or training sessions on each assignment.

### Equipment
Your own exclusive telephone line, with clean order book, notebook attached, and access to as many telephone directories as possible. (Collect old ones from other people's dustbins; they're better than nothing.)

### Premises
It's important to have your telephone in a quiet place in your home. Council tenants could *not* be prosecuted for using a private telephone for business, though some busybody might gossip about it, so be discreet!

### Write to
The list of firms which might give you employment is long. Try: Sales Force Ltd., 1–2 Berners Street, London W1P 3AG (Tel: 01-637 1444). A lot depends on where you live. 'Those in major

conurbations enjoy greater continuity,' says Sales Force Ltd.

**Law**
No legal restrictions apply.

**Advertising**
Your nice voice and manner are the best advertisement.

**What you can earn**
Earnings average between £2.50 and £3.50 an hour, which includes the cost of *local* calls only. *All* non-local call charges are reimbursed at cost. Pay is on the basis of a fixed amount per effective call. Sales Force add: 'Some girls are in their third year of an ongoing campaign requiring 50 calls a week; other campaigns are covered by 20 girls making 200 calls a week.'

**Advantages**
It's convenient – you need not leave the house or flat where you live.

**Disadvantages**
How can you ever go out shopping?

## *Tourist guide*   M/F   30–60

### *(or escort)*

Some investment for training. Good income for the qualified. Fascinating work for the less qualified also. Can be done from home as casual, temporary or part-time work but only for people who enjoy travelling about.

**Qualifications**
Good general education standard. You must pass an examination set by the London Transport Board (L.T.B.) which involves a part-time course which runs from September to March. Application forms for the 1981/2 course become available in May/June 1981. The training course is one evening a week and the whole of every Saturday (Saturdays are mostly spent out at Museums, etc.). The examination is in three parts, Written, Oral and in a Museum. You should be reasonably fluent in at least one foreign language. You get a Blue Badge on passing the examination final. You can however become an escort without any of the above qualifications.

**Training**
Some coach tour operators or tourist firms give their own training. However, the best way to become a trained and fully qualified tourist guide is to take the course and examination set by the London Transport Board.

**How to train**
Cost of the L.T.B. course at present is £200. But you could be taken on by a Coach tour operator firm as an escort and work your way up; this would mean that if you suited the work they might subsidise you by helping you to pay for the L.T.B. course to become a proper tourist guide with Blue Badge. (However, Ilsa French of the L.T.B. warns me that the work of an escort is 'exhausting, mundane things, at least at first, like meeting people at airports and taking them to hotels.' All good experience for the real thing later!)

**Equipment**
Your health and strength, a nice manner with people, a liking for and interest in subjects such as history, architecture, etc.

**Premises**
Obviously this is outside work which can only be done *from* home, but it can be done in short spurts, so that you get home every few hours if you work locally.

**Write to**
The Guide Activities Department, London Transport Board, 26 Gros-

venor Gardens, London SW1 (Tel: 01-730 3450). Also try: Mr Ken Taylor, Thomas Cook – Peterborough (Tel: 01-493 7080); address Thos. Cook Group Ltd., P.O. Box 36, Thorpe Wood, Peterborough, PE3 6SB.

## Law

Also write to and become a member of the professional body, the Guild of Guides and Lecturers, who fix rates of payment and look after the legal and cultural side. At present, regional membership is £9 per annum and London membership £32.50. Write to the Secretary-General, Mrs. Helen Clapp, Guild of Guides and Lecturers, 7 Blackfriars Lane, London EC4V 6ER (Tel: 01-248 7752).

## Advertising

You will see these jobs advertised in the quality newspapers, magazines and on University or Polytechnic notice-boards; or you can yourself advertise your services.

## What you can earn

The present rate for a qualified guide is £25 per day, inclusive of expenses. The present rate for an unqualified escort is, of course, much lower and is negotiated between the escort and his coach employers. The rate may be somewhat higher for unsocial hours, but a great deal of an escort's work takes place at unsocial hours anyway, for instance meeting holidaymakers at dawn or midnight at airports or stations.

Rates of pay are fixed by the Guild of Guides and Lecturers, so it is beneficial to join for 'improvement of working conditions, widening liaison, off-season activities and the monthly mailing calendar or Newsletter with news of legal protection and all activities, inclusive.'

## Advantages

Ideal for the lonely or isolated person who wants to meet new, interesting people from abroad; to make new friends and influence people. Also you can travel abroad at your employer's expense.

## Disadvantages

If you fancied getting away from it all . . . far from Britain and the British, and then got sent to the Costa Brava, you might feel a bit frustrated. . . .

## *Toy-maker*  M/F  18–60

Some investment, similar in scale to dressmaking. Income is also more or less in line with sewing for a living. Can be done at home, either as a home-worker for a manufacturer or you can try and design and make your own ideas.

## Qualifications

You need a skill in sewing and an ability to use a sewing-machine and to cut out patterns. Some skill in subjects like painting and drawing. Ability to do machining of soft toys, paint toy soldiers or to dress dolls.

## Training

Get ideas from *The Good Toy Guide*, published by the Toy Libraries Association, available for £2.95 plus 35p postage and packing from the Toy Libraries Association, Seabrook House, Darkes Lane, Potters Bar, Herts. Perhaps experience in a toy factory is best, where you can get your training free.

## How to train

Your local Adult Education Institute will probably have training courses in upholstery, dressmaking, arts and crafts and all these subjects will help you to learn how to make toys. The firms listed here sometimes send someone to your home to show you how they want the work done, or they send you samples to study or copy.

Visit Madame Tussaud's and ask their expert to recommend some guidance in the form of books, pictures or classes.

## Equipment
Sewing-machine and all the attachments described in the upholstery and dressmaking chapters. A child's box of paints would be useful; also transfers, patterns, plasticine, gum and as much of a do-it-yourself carpentry kit as you can afford to buy.

## Premises
A workroom at home, with childproof baskets or boxes.

## Write to
Here are some of the toy manufacturers who employ home workers: H. Schelhorn & Co. Ltd, Cobden House, Cobden Street, Leicester LE1 2LB (Tel: Leicester (0533) 23334); for soft toys, teddy bears and rag dolls, Gwentoys Ltd, Pontnewyndd Industrial Estate, Pontypool, Gwent NP4 6YY (Tel: Pontypool (049 55) 4881); for die-cast and plastic toys, Britains Ltd, Blackhorse Lane, Walthamstow, London, E17 5QD (Tel: 01-527 0041). Also ask the British Toy Manufacturing Association for names of firms all over Britain employing home workers. The Association's new address is 80 Camberwell Road, London SE5.

## Law
Consult the C.A.B. about any regulations that might apply to home-made toys; e.g. paint, stuffing.

If you are working at home for a manufacturer, then the work comes under the Toy Manufacturing Wages Council; it lays down in its Orders that the statutory rates are the minimum that can apply both to factory workers and to homeworkers. This is a protection for you as home toy-maker and means that you should not be exploited over payment.

The Association say: 'The Wages Inspectorate is charged with the duty in the course of its inspections of establishing that the employers comply with the requirements of the Wages Council and, following a meeting of the Administrative Committee of the Wages Council, it has recently been reported that the Inspectorate has found no substantial infringements of the Order.'

## Advertising
If you are designing and making your own toys, start by advertising locally and letting local shops, boutiques, know of your work.

## What you can earn
This work has not been highly paid in the past, but as you can see from the above, it is now controlled by law.

## Advantages
It could be creative work, if you have the imagination to design your own puppets and a whole range of new toys.

## Disadvantages
Perhaps it's not a trade to depend upon during hard times.

---

# Translator  M/F  19–90

Investment in a Language Course might be expensive. Income is lower than it ought to be for this skill but has improved in recent years. Can be done at home.

## Qualifications
Knowledge of languages alone is not enough – to use them commercially, you need other skills such as secretarial ability, some technical or scientific

knowledge. (I speak from personal experience – I started out in life as a translator with a fair smattering of German, Russian and French. I think you need mostly luck in this trade; that is luck to meet the right people, or the right firm who needs your knowledge.)

## Training
The Information Officer of the Institute of Linguists says: 'It is possible to learn languages from tapes or records and those put out by the B.B.C., the Linguaphone Institute and the World of Learning are particularly good. Normally the more expensive the course, the better it is. Courses that are combined with a text book are more likely to be of use than those which simply have lesson sheets.'

## How to train
The Institute says: 'Unfortunately there are no official requirements as to qualifications for translators and ad hoc interpreters. This situation means that there are a great many people doing work of rather poor quality at a very low fee. However, the Institute say that there are now four separate kinds of membership of the Institute, from students under 25, £3.50 per annum, to highest class fellowship for the fully qualified, who give proof of study and examination status, £20 per annum.

'Most freelance translators and interpreters work through translation agencies since it is extremely difficult to find clients directly. Naturally the rates of pay are lower, but there is slightly more chance of getting a regular flow of work since it may well come from several sources. Translation agencies are usually listed in the classified pages of the telephone directory or can be contacted through the local Chamber of Commerce.'

*Note:* This is all perfectly true. But speaking as one who had to make a living at home with no other equipment than a secondhand typewriter and some knowledge of languages and a few old dictionaries, I can only say that I never went near an agency but I did make a reasonable living. The way I chose was to write to all the factories near to my home where I knew or guessed that they either used or bought or sold foreign machinery. I asked for translation work and was soon overwhelmed with specifications and blueprints to be translated for fitting or using machine-tools, cutting-tools, electrical furnace equipment and so on. I visited the various factories and asked the factory-hands to tell me the authentic *English* word for each piece of machinery. Then I sought its equivalent in dictionaries or from experts. I recommend this method, but I agree that the work is not well paid. The reason is that Britain has a large contingent of immigrants of every nationality who have greater skill at languages than any native-born Britain can learn . . . except by years abroad or at University.

## Equipment
Any old typewriter will do. Dictionaries (as many as possible) and a good library nearby.

## Write to
The Institute of Linguists, 24a Highbury Grove, London N5 2EA (Tel: 01-359 7445). For more literary work, try writing for advice to the Translators' Association of the Society of Authors, 84 Drayton Gardens, London SW10 (Tel: 01-373 6642). They produce a useful leaflet about copyright and other tips for literary translators.

## Law
No restrictions whatsoever.

## Advertising
Try the newsagent's window; try advertising in papers and magazines like the *New Statesman*, *Spectator* etc. And try my personal advice of writing to individual firms and offering to put

85

their foreign correspondence into good, reliable, reasonable English (or vice versa).

**What you can earn**
Ad hoc interpreting rates for main European languages (business, industrial and court interpreting etc): whole day (7 hours): £25 to £30; half day (3 hours) £25; hourly £10 (depending on nature of duties in each case). These fees do not include expenses.

Translation work fees in 1976 ranged from roughly £20 to £25 per 1,000 words for a straightforward text to £25 to £35 per 1,000 words of a specialist nature.

There is more money to be made in translating nowadays because there is greater demand owing to the Common Market. If you work for a foreign firm or customer, you can charge for hospitality and even gifts on your income tax returns. (See also *Tourist guide*, page 82.)

**Advantages**
The point about this work is that like typing manuscripts etc, it is good business if you can get it because it's all pure profit. An old machine, paper, carbons and a typewriter ribbon are your only equipment; so it's a good investment for *regular* work.

**Disadvantages**
For some reason I can't explain a translator in the United Kingdom has a fairly low professional status. Probably because although in principle you should be university-trained, anyone who's lived, say, a year abroad and has a flair for language can do it.

---

## *Tupperware hostess*   F   20–40

---

Investment nil. Income fair to good, but variable. Can be done at home or at a friend's house.

**Qualifications**
A nice smile and friendly manner. You should be a relaxed housewife who likes socialising.

**Training**
The beginner housewife attends a Tupperware party to see how the party is done. She is then trained by attending three or four Tupperware parties with a Tupperware manager.

**How to train**
She is given a display case of Tupperware and the manager helps her to arrange her first parties. I will quote what Tupperware (The International name in Polythene Housewares) told me:

'Demonstrating Tupperware at morning, afternoon or evening Tupperware parties is pleasant part-time work and one meets interesting people in friendly suroundings. The Tupperware dealer makes her own hours and can earn £12 to £15 a week clear, demonstrating two to three Tupperware parties a week. She fixes the time of parties with her hostesses at their convenience. There is no cash outlay to become a Tupperware dealer. Generally the sales from the first party clear her display case.

'Further training is given regularly to keep everyone up to date on new items and new ideas. There are attractive incentive prizes to be won by dealers.'

Well, that's what they say. They also add that there are chances to work on a full-time basis earning £60 a week upwards, possibly leading to a managership.

**Premises**
You, clearly, need a house with rooms large enough for all this party-giving (and some clothes to match!).

**Write to**
The Tupperware Company, Tupperware House, 43 Upper Grosvenor Street, London W1V 0BE (Tel: 01-629 7861). Or ring Tupperware House at the above number for the name and telephone number of your nearest Tupperware Distributor for further information.

**Law**
No restrictions.

**Advertising**
All done socially, by word of mouth or over the telephone.

**What you can earn**
The money (quoted above) sounds all right, provided you don't get bored with all those parties . . .

**Advantages**
You make a lot of friends. No more lonely housewife stuff!

**Disadvantages**
You might wish for a week without a party? You might run out of people to invite!

---

## *Tutor*   M/F   18–40

### *(correspondence school or private coach)*

No investment necessary. Good income. Can be done at home.

**Qualifications**
To work as a part-time, home-based tutor it is essential to be qualified by degree, by professional qualification, or some acceptable alternative. Teaching experience is helpful and welcomed, while in the technological fields practical workshop or laboratory experience is of great importance.

**Training**
Tutoring by correspondence means you must be fit to give tuition in an individual subject under the following headings:- General Education, University and Higher Education, Professional, Commercial and Technical.

**How to train**
See under 'Qualifications' above. Also start your own 'coaching' class. To get advice ring 'Brass Tacks' (see *Useful Contacts*).

**Equipment**
Writing materials, a desk in a reasonably quiet room. Subject and reference books.

**Premises**
At home, as above.

**Write to**
The Education Department of your Local Authority; The Secretary at your Local Polytechnic, or even try your nearest Comprehensive School. Try an Independent School, University Registrar, the Open University or one of the many Correspondence Colleges. Also write to: The Council for the Accreditation of Correspondence Colleges, 27 Marylebone Road, London NW1 5JS (Tel: 01-935 5391). Try also: Mr. A. Spencer, International Correspondence Schools, Intertext House, Stewarts Road, London SW8 4UJ (Tel: 01-622 9911). Colleges maintain registers of would-be tutors.

**Law**
No restrictions

**Advertising**
Most Correspondence Colleges have a waiting list (or reserve panel) of potential tutors, especially in the more popular subjects. Thus very few newspaper advertisements for such tutors will be seen and you must approach suitable colleges on the off-chance.

### What you can earn
Most of the work is sent out for marking and correction. Fees paid vary according to subject and level. Tutors are generally remunerated on a *per capita* rate. The number of hours a tutor devotes to this work is normally fixed by mutual negotiation and consent, but the Association tell me that few colleges would generally allow more than, say, 20 hours a week.

### Advantages
Clearly, this is nice work if you can get it.

### Disadvantages
I notice that the limit set – probably of 20 hours a week – must limit your earnings.

### Comment
Coaching is more or less the same, but pupils are visited. Rates vary; advertise locally, contact agencies for work.

## *Typist*  M/F  16–70

No investment. Really good income. Can be done at home.

### Qualifications
Ability to type fast and accurately, and knowledge of how to lay out commercial work (e.g. business letters, invoices ) or technical matter (e.g. reports, data) or literature (e.g. novels and plays). Do them all if you can.

### Training
Buy, beg or borrow a typewriter and practise until proficient. Go to night-class or commercial school. Some schools now teach typing to final year pupils.

### How to train
Experience is your best teacher. Take on every job that's offered . . . you'll soon be fast and accurate. (Learn touch-typing if possible.)

### Equipment
Typewriter, paper, carbon, reading-lamp.

### Premises
At home, any room in the house, kitchen, bedroom or study.

### Write to
Type out some good, very brief letters offering your typing services; do each one separately; do at least a dozen a day to get started. Then deliver them either by post or by hand to local firms, shops, factories in your immediate neighbourhood. One very bright housewife I know had some cards printed calling herself a 'secretarial agency' and dropped them through the letter-box of various local firms, offering efficient (shorthand) typing at short notice for £2 an hour plus petrol, and was overwhelmed with work. She claims it's made her rich!

Remember: your best customers may turn out to be small shops and small businesses who cannot afford a full-time secretary. It depends where you live. If you live way out in the country, offer typing help to farmers of course, but try for the bigger jobs like typing books and novels. Write to dozens of publishing firms whom you will find listed in the *Writers' & Artists' Year Book* in your local reference library.

Also write to the following for work: Success-after-Sixty (Office Employment) Ltd, 14 Great Castle Street, London W1N 8JU (Tel: 01-580 8035). Also offer your typing services as a 'temp' for one or two hours per day or per week. But work for yourself and *not* for an agency who get most of the money!

**Law**
No restrictions.

**Advertising**
As soon as you've started to earn something, put advertisements in magazines like the *New Statesman*, *Spectator*, *New Society* etc. Put a card in your newsagent's window.

**What you can earn**
The rates vary. Payment is usually per thousand words. Telephone a typing agency and ask what their charges are and that should serve you as some guide. Remember that copy typing work that is already clearly typed and set out is easier than typing from someone's handwriting and you make your charges accordingly. If you can type faster than 80 or 90 words per minute, you should earn a good living. My friend's rate of £2 an hour is, I think, rather too low.

**Advantages**
This is one of the easier jobs to combine with running a home.

**Disadvantages**
Some people can't stand all that tapping noise . . . so smile sweetly at the neighbours and keep on the right side of them!

---

# *Upholsterer* M/F 18–60

---

This is not cheap to start. It helps to have a sewing-machine of your own, and you will need up to £200 approximately for secondhand tools and materials. High income. Can be done at home, or by visiting clients, or by working freelance for another upholsterer.

**Qualifications**
Three-year apprenticeship or attendance at an upholstery evening class in any Adult Education College, usually one evening class a week for 2 or 3 years.

**Training**
Should include training in making curtains and loose covers as well as upholstered furniture.

**How to train**
There are Upholstery Schools which run full-time courses; there are also evening classes available from Technical Schools and Local Authorities. Ask you local Council, or try asking a local furniture shop or store for advice on finding upholstery evening classes or a teacher. Contact 'Brass Tacks' (ring 01-249 9462) between 1 p.m. and 5 p.m.

They plan to hold open evenings when local residents can use the workshop's tools and facilities to do their own household repairs under expert supervision. Try your local 'Brass Tacks' shop to learn upholstery also.

**Equipment**
You could manage with your own ordinary sewing machine in order to make curtains and loose covers. But for more ambitious upholstery work, you would need to buy a larger workroom machine with attachments. You also need to buy (secondhand if possible) upholsterer's hammer, shears with a blunt nose, various needles and springs and things like frames. Obviously, you'll need linings, canvas, webbing, hair, down or feathers, calico, flock, wadding, castors and sundries which include tacks, twine, studs, gimp, fringe, flexibead etc. (say £150 to £200 to buy secondhand tools and your basic materials).

The Head of the Crafts Department (I.L.E.A.) of the Addison Adult Education Institute, Addison Gardens, London W14 0DT (Tel: 01-603 6102) says he thinks you need only between £25 and £100 for upholstery tools; but for restoration of antique furniture, £100 to £150 for a complete set of tools, dyes, polishes etc. For upholsterers' warehousemen stock tools, try Messrs. Porter Nicholson Ltd, Portland House, Norlington Road, E10, and D. L. Forster Ltd, 17 Tramway Avenue, E.15.

## Premises
Any room will do, but you need space to store your materials and equipment. Have a good worktable, well-lit, and shelves or cupboards placed high where your tools can be kept out of the reach of children.

## Write to
The Administrative Secretary of The Association of Master Upholsterers (this is a national organisation), Dormar House, Mitre Bridge, Scrubs Lane, London NW10 6QX (Tel: 01-205 0465). Membership of the Association is open to crafts-people running their own business. The monthly bulletin is circulated only to members. Membership fees vary from £12 for the self-employed or several employees to £15 for 3, 4 or 5 employees. For advice on learning upholstery, ask Fred Johnson of 'Brass Tacks' (see *Useful Contacts*.)

## Law
This depends on the sort of district you live in and the amount of business you do. Most upholsteresses who become out-workers for a firm of upholsterers or for furniture-makers do not need permission from their Local Authority.

But if you live in a high-class residential road and you are upholstering whole suites of furniture which will be not only visible but even may cause a traffic obstruction when the furniture van comes to collect your work . . . then it might be advisable to send a letter to the Planning Department of your Town Hall or call or telephone to say you want to mention you are doing some work for Messrs so-and-so and you'd like to have their blessing. If in doubt as to what you should do, go to your nearest C.A.B. office for advice.

## Advertising
Advertise in your local paper or contact upholsterers in your area through Yellow Pages. The monthly bulletin of the Association of Master Upholsterers also carries such advertisements. Don't forget to put a card in the local newsagent's window as well.

## What you can earn
This work is well paid. If you are good at it and can put in enough hours, you can make very good money indeed.

## Advantages
There is usually plenty of work both in town and country. Satisfying, creative work too.

## Disadvantages
You must be able to maintain high standards and keep schedules; and some people dislike the noise of a sewing-machine.

---

## *Window cleaner* M/F 18–35

---

Small investment for tools, high earner for hard work. Can be done near your home.

## Qualifications
Health and strength and a good reputation locally.

## Training
Best training is experience of cleaning

work (see page 21) or looking after your own home.

## How to train
This is very independent work, so you could choose any way of training that suits you. Join a local team for a day to see if the work is too hard. This work is now popular for women as well as men, like gardening (see page 37),

where women are sometimes preferred.

## Equipment
Buckets, detergents, brushes, cloths, a 'squeegee' (which makes work easy) and a ladder. A push-cart if you have no car.

## Premises
Work as near as possible to your own home, preferably in districts where you are well-known. Some householders have, alas, been burgled by freelance window-cleaners, and are nervous of them. On the other hand window-cleaners in most towns are in great demand (like gardeners) because there are too few of them and often too expensive. So try to build up a regular connection. Shops are, of course, easier work, with groundfloor cleaning.

## Write to
Your Insurance brokers first. You will have to pay a much higher life-insurance premium. Also to your Local Authority asking for work.

## Law
You must insure anyone helping you with the work.

## Advertising
Newsagent's card, personal cards, Local Authority references, shops etc.

## What you can earn
Try not to work for less than £2.50 per hour minimum. Vary your prices according to district, house, windows, etc.

## Advantages
Work only when you feel like it.

## Disadvantages
Bad weather is bad news for you. Also I am told by window-cleaners they take on too much work per day, earn a good living but quickly get worn out.

# *Writer* M/F 14–84

No investment. High income if successful. No income if not successful. Can be done at home.

## Qualifications
Writing talent in one or more of the following areas: documentary, romance, thrillers, fiction, technical work, broadcasting and/or TV, children's books, history and biography, poetry or drama.

## Training
If you have no talent, or very little, you are wasting your time, because you won't earn anything at all.

An agent will not take you on unless he thinks he can place your work. You do not necessarily need writing talent for the technical work or even for documentaries (some would add romance and thrillers!). But you need to study hard and learn the rules for this kind of writing, and to be acquainted with the relevant field for technical and documentary.

One way of testing whether you have any qualification for writing is to sit down and write an essay or article or story which you think might be suitable for publication. (Do not send it anywhere; this is just a self-testing exercise.) If you have written it very simply (as though you were writing a letter to Grandma or to 'Any Answers') without any fine phrases or big words and yet have made it vivid and interesting, you may have some talent which could be developed by study and work. More important than writing style is to have something individual to say. Never copy anyone else.

## How to train

Do not attempt to write fiction. Even if you are a genius, nobody wants it, and the years spent in trying to get it published will harm your morale and will make money only for the Post Office, who will be busy for years returning your ms. Do not waste time or money reading how-to-write manuals. Instead study the work of successful writers. The quickest way to make money from writing is to write a good thriller, but this requires a great deal of technical knowledge and research.

## Equipment

A good typewriter (I think a radio is useful too).

## Premises

A comfortable armchair.

## Write to

Get copies of the B.B.C. paperbacks with useful advice, e.g. *Writing for the B.B.C.* (A new edition has recently been prepared.) This is supplied by B.B.C. Publications, 35 Marylebone High Street, London W1M 4AA. Also get a free pamphlet called *Notes on Radio Drama* from the B.B.C. Radio Drama Department, Broadcasting House, London W1A 1AA.

If you decide to write romance, try it on publishers Mills and Boon (address in the London telephone book). To find publishers, agents, etc., get the *Writers' and Artists' Year Book* from your local reference library.

## Law

If you write a documentary, a biography, history or technical work, either you or your publisher should have the finished ms inspected by a lawyer (for possible libel or copyright problem).

## Advertising

I suppose it's been done . . . but I wouldn't ever advise it.

## What you can earn

Almost the only Writers (apart from journalists which is something quite different) who make money in the sense of making a living are the thriller and romance writers who turn out possibly two, three or even more novels every year. With the exception of a few (very few) top-rank, world-famous writers who make a substantial living, all the rest would not be able to support a home, family and other commitments unless they received large sums of money from other sources, e.g. radio, television, lecturing, free trips abroad for personal appearances on foreign networks etc, etc.

## Advantages

Often the people most handicapped by life have the greatest success in the writing profession. This may be because the restrictions of reality cause them to lead a far more intense, imaginative life than other people.

## Disadvantages

Writing is much harder work than, say, cleaning a 3-storey house from top to bottom and even more exhausting physically as well as mentally and emotionally. Keeping your bottom stuck to that armchair can become the hardest exercise of the lot.

## *Yoga teacher*   M/F   6–60 *(to learn)*, 20–70 *(to teach)*

No investment except in training, lessons etc. Modest regular income. Can be done at home.

## Qualifications

Enthusiasm, dedication, patience, seriousness. Some talent for gymnastics, dancing is a help. The ability to teach and/or communicate.

## Training

Your local Education Department

probably provides residential course or other day or evening classes.

## How to train
Where to get lessons to train as Yoga teacher, get details from The Secretary, *'The Rambler'*, 22 New Road, Sandhurst, Camberley, Surrey, GU17 8EF. Or buy a monthly magazine: *Yoga Today*. Send self-addressed and stamped envelope to P.O. Box 1, Barking, Essex, IG11 8AZ.

Other books include *Teaching Yoga* by Donald G. Butler, £5.25; *Keeping up with Yoga* by Lyn Marshall, £1.25; *Yoga 28-day Exercise Plan* by Richard Hittleman, £5.50.

## Equipment
You need a warm, empty room at home. (See *Dance Teacher*, page 26). Any loose-fitting dress will do or have leotards, ballet practice outfit.

## Premises
At home. If you have neighbours on the floor below, make friends with them; invite them to a free class. Be discreet, nice.

## Write to
Write to find out about officially-recognised diplomas for this work from the Secretary of *The Rambler* (as above).

## Advertising
You will have seen many advertisements in the more intellectual magazines, cards in newsagents etc.

## Law
No restrictions but advisable to consult C.A.B. and *The Rambler*.

## What you can earn
I can only give the price of lessons three years ago. A woman friend in Brighton had three previous teachers of Yoga who were highly qualified (which is very necessary in order to teach!). They held classes in their own homes at 75p per person an hour. Hylda tells me 'the classes were always full'.

## Advantages
If you enjoy sitting in the so-called Lotus position, you can actually earn a reasonably good living nowadays by having a whole class full of pupil 'lotus-eaters'!

## Disadvantages
I know some very great artists like violinist Mr Menuhin do it regularly and get benefit. But standing on one's head is not really the purpose of this book – even to earn a living!

*Part Two*

Part Two

# How to set about it

*(by Ann and Katy who are introduced in this Chapter.)*

Your choice of job should be directly linked with the neighbourhood where you live (town or country, residential or commercial) as well as with your family circumstances.

Try and discover what your district lacks; then discover how best you could commercially provide it.

Decide how much you want to earn. Clearly there's no quick fortune to be made cleaning, telephone-answering or envelope-writing, whereas you could get comfortably rich quite quickly if you're a trained chiropodist or upholsterer, a fast typist, a cookery expert, an open-market stall holder; if you've got a few goats or rabbits then you should already be making money. You must be prepared for hard work and some initial investment.

Decide how much you can afford to spend on the equipment you need to do the job. If you have no money, decide what the chances are of getting a loan. (All this is dealt with in the next chapter under Organising, where you will be able to follow throughout what Ann and Katy did.)

Decide whether anyone is likely to object; for example, what would neighbours say if you suddenly turned the spare bedroom into a dancing school?

Decide what name you will use for your business; your own? Or will you think of a new one?

There are a number of ways to organise depending on your home circumstances and the job you choose.

All these problems, in just this order, faced the two clear-headed business women I have chosen to tell their stories. They started with no business experience whatsoever but the first thing they had to do was to organise themselves. So now read on.

**Mrs. Kate Barr**, aged 31, married, two children under six, lives in town, in a large old Victorian house converted into flats. Her husband is a male nurse at a local hospital.

Kate chose upholstery, having studied two terms at night class in the local Institute of Adult Education.

Kate said: 'I'm good with a needle. Then I got hooked on upholstery soft furnishings, curtains. There's more money in it than dressmaking.'

She added: 'While at evening class two nights a week, I furnished our entire flat which meant we could afford much nicer materials than if I'd bought from shops.'

**Ann Aston**, aged 40, single, lives alone in a cottage on the outskirts of town, near a big common with trees. Ann, alone since her mother died, has had no training at all. She owns her own home and has started a teas/refreshments business.

Ann said: 'People were always stopping their cars outside my garden and shouting over the hedge, "Do you do teas?".'

She decided: 'One Sunday morning I made piles of scones and fancy cakes. If no one came, I thought they won't be wasted because I could pop them into the freezer and eat them myself later on.'

97

# Business techniques

No accountant can look after your petty cash book for you or keep your expenses up to date; if he did he wouldn't be your accountant, he'd be a Director of your firm drawing as much salary as you are, or probably more!

Kate and Ann found this part of the job simple and easy.

All you need is a pencil and paper.

## First day of business

*Kate:*
'I went out and bought a voucher block for my daily expenses, two notebooks, some carbon paper, pen and pencil.'

*Ann*
'I wrote everything down on two pieces of paper. After a few days, I had to buy an exercise book with lined pages to try and get some sort of order.'

## Petty Cash

*Kate*
'I wrote my first page of the voucher block like this':

*Date.*

| | |
|---|---:|
| Bus fare and return home from stationery shop | 75p |
| Cost of voucher block | 35p |
| Cost of pen and pencil | 25p |
| Carbon paper (5 at 6p each) | 30p |
| 2 notebooks at 40p each | 80p |
| Today's expenses | £2.45p |

*Ann*
'The accountant told me to keep at least two notebooks for him. I marked one "cash book" and in it I recorded all bank transactions. I marked the other "Petty cash" and I put the small cash transactions, mainly my expenses, into it.

'I put all moneys received into a till and banked them daily. I divided my cash book into 4 columns, showing Sales, Sundries, Insurance, Total.'

# Expenses

### Kate

'The voucher block is small enough to fit into my handbag. I write all my outgoings on it immediately before I forget: stamps, bus fares, telephones, every time I buy petrol for business, new needles and thread for my sewing machine etc. I write in the total at night and I pop it back into my handbag.

'Then every Saturday I make a free hour in the afternoon, and copy everything from the voucher block into my petty cash book, sales book and so on. This helps me to see how I'm doing, by balancing my overheads against income.'

### Ann

'I was too busy baking scones and making tea for customers to keep a daily account of my expenses. The result was that I got into a fearful muddle; when the accountant wanted a daily record of my expenses I had to try and remember, using the rough notes I'd kept. I know I forgot a lot of small items and that's why I made an actual loss the first year. Now I keep my books in good order by working at them every Sunday evening.'

---

# Claims against tax

### Kate

'Every April I total up the Petty Cash Book and claim this against tax. It includes all my expenses for the workroom including, light, heat and cleaning; travel expenses, cost of a charwoman three times a week; cost of a babysitter when necessary; cost of all business phone calls, insurance, mortgage, car depreciation, sewing machine depreciation, cost of special upholstery journals and patterns; my travel and hotel expenses for attending the annual meeting of an upholstery society, the cost of an evening dress for this occasion. All these bills, including water rates and rates, I clip inside my cash books and send them, duly added up and totalled, to the accountant in April each year. He fixes a proportion of each item which he thinks I ought to claim.' (See 'Tax extra' later in this section.)

### Ann

'I had no tax to pay for several years because I claimed for the building work and refurnishing the house. I now put all bills and receipts into separate boxes. I found that the important thing is to keep my Petty Cash and Cash Book up to date and never let it get more than a few days behind.

'Now that I employ casual labour in the summer, I also keep a wages book and I get my girls to sign each week for their wages, and that serves as a receipt. As they are "casual" I don't have to worry about insurance for them. But the law demands that I give the authorities the names of those I employ to prevent exploitation.'

# Book-keeping

*Kate*

'There's only one right way. I suppose because I was in business before I married, I got into good habits! I keep my order book open by the phone; pinned to it is my Petty Cash book. The thing is to enter everything immediately into the Petty Cash book. Or I jot it down on a bit of paper wherever I am, even standing by the gas-stove, put it into my purse, and then enter it next day in Petty Cash. The thing to remember is this; work is quite hard enough without the awful hardship of trying to remember every little thing. But it's those little things which make all the difference between your making a profit or a loss at years' end. If you can't remember all your expenses, then use your imagination a bit! Better still keep a little voucher with you wherever you go, even if that's out on the tiles one night, when you had to give a customer a lift home in a taxi. Even a short taxi ride nowadays cost about a pound.

'In my desk I keep order pad, cash book, petty cash book, cheque book (business account), cheque book (personal account), bank giro credit book for paying-in, folder for invoices, folder for receipts.

'Round about the third week in April, I make up a big parcel for the accountant, containing my voucher blocks, Petty Cash book totalled, Cash Book totalled, 2 folders containing invoices/receipts, business account cheque stubs and the bank giro paying-in book.'

*Ann*

'I follow much the same procedure as Kate but it's just not possible for me to enter my purchases immediately. I have to keep in big stocks of things like flour, tea, sugar, butter and now ice-cream, cigarettes and sweets. (I had to get a separate licence for cigarettes and sweets.) These are weekly purchases and there's far too much to enter into my Purchase Account Book; it would take up too much of my time in one go. So I take the bills and invoices and clip them together in a file-box. I try to make one Sunday a month the day for entering them in my Purchases book. But my last season was such a roaring success I never got round to it. I had to leave it all to the accountant when he came and I let him take the boxes away with him. You see I can't leave the shop now!

'Besides I've got to keep far more books than Kate Barr. Apart from Purchases, I've got a Wages Book with casual payments to two regular cleaners, one handyman, six waitresses etc.

'As I'm usually in the shop or cafe to receive customers, my accountant lets me claim for weekly shampoo, cosmetics and manicure as well as a proportion of my clothing. So I keep all my receipts, or as many as I can remember and I enter these into my Petty Cash book. So the total at the end of the year is rather terrific. It frightens me just to look at it!'

# Duplicating

*Kate*

'One thing the accountant taught me was always to keep copies of everything. If you have to send a receipt or an invoice to be checked always keep a copy. Keep the original safely for your own book-keeping. Carbon copies are the cheapest way. But if you send important receipts through the post for examination by the Tax Office or the accountant, have a photostat made locally.'

*Ann*

'I even make three copies of everything now. One for the accountant, one for the files and one for the record in case anything gets lost. It's better than the time-wasting job of having to search for missing documents.'

# Letters and phone calls

*Kate*

'I enter both these in my Petty Cash as I do them; no danger of forgetting them. Mind you – now that the telephone charges are so high, I've had to learn the proper business technique of telephoning.' (See how to make a telephone call, in the next section.)

*Ann*

'I'm bound to keep these to the barest minimum. I don't have time for either.

The only phone calls I encourage are from local schoolgirls on holiday who want to do a few hours waitressing or baking.'

*Kate*

'Next comes the organising. I found it wasn't too bad if you take it in stages.'

*Ann*

'The important thing is to write it down as you go along.'

# *Organising*

### Kate
'I started in upholstery, making to order from customers' materials, covering armchairs, easy chairs, settees or suites, making loose covers, soft furnishings, curtains, cushions, and so on.'

### Ann
'I chose teas/refreshments, as making scones and cakes is about all I could ever do. But the cottage is quite picturesque, with a lawn and a flagged pathway and it is just off a main north-south roadway.'

## How much do I need to invest?

### Kate
'I needed £175. This would buy me a larger, secondhand workroom sewing machine for £100 and left £75 for tools, including special needles, an upholster's hammer, shears with a blunt nose and regular spring needles. Until I could raise the money, however, my own sewing machine had to do and it is perfectly suitable for the simpler work.'

### Ann
'I started with almost nothing in the way of equipment. By summer I needed about £1,000 to buy new china, iron-and-plastic tables and chairs and to make some alterations to the house.'

## Do I need permission

### Kate
'I asked at the Adult Education Institute where I studied and they said that I did not need anyone's permission. However, I hoped to earn a substantial income and to claim certain overhead expenses against income tax. So, to be on the safe side, I informed the Local Authority I was going to use at least one room for my work, and that put me in the clear. I also discussed it with C.A.B., and they said, remember to be discreet and not have great vans standing outside the house!'

### Ann
'I didn't even realise I needed anyone's permission but when I saw the C.A.B. to get the name of an accountant, they warned me about the Food Hygiene Act also. So in the end I had to get permission from the Planning Officer and from the Environmental Health Department to get my premises registered for providing food to the public. They claim a right to inspect my premises regularly but after the initial visit, no one ever came again.'

# What can I earn

*Kate*
'I already earn nearly three times the permitted sum (£1,375 is the sum you can earn without paying tax) because I started making up materials for one of the Institute teachers while I was still learning. He has an upholstery business. I could earn double that again but I told the Council Man I would not let the business get too big.'

*Ann*
'My business depends a lot on the weather, though even in winter I do a regular trade indoors in coffees, minerals, cigarettes and toasted snacks. My new accountant advised me to get a licence to sell cigarettes, ices, sweets and other things for the quiet season. In summer I have to employ casual labour.'

# Business name

*Kate*
'I used my own name "Kate Barr". It's my dream one day to make artistic items of small furniture and have my name on them.'

*Ann*
'I use the name "The White Forge" which is what my house is known as (it was an old forge hundreds of years ago). I registered this with the Registrar of Business Names, and this cost £1.'

*Note:* New proposals to replace the register with legal requirements to display relevant company information on premises and business documents are at present being considered by the Government.

# Business premises

*Kate*
'I asked C.A.B. for advice on how to approach the Council. They telephoned and made an appointment for me to visit the Planning Officer, in the Planning Department. He said he was pleased I'd come to see him as our flat was in a strictly residential area. Later a letter arrived from him saying they'd no objection provided I checked my legal contract with my landlord, which I did.' (See under 'Law'.)

*Ann*
'I didn't realise the bye-laws were so strict about selling food to the public. I had a visit from the Health Officer; he approved the kitchen but advised me to have a lavatory and washroom installed alongside the indoor cafe.'

Ann was also told she ought to have obtained Council approval before putting up a 'Teas' sign. 'In the end, a nice man was sent along to make the sign and to hang it up for me, high up in some treetops. So it's visible from quite a distance without being an eyesore.'

## Do I need an accountant?

### Kate

Kate discussed this with her husband. 'We telephoned to the Small Firms Information Centre for advice. We didn't know whether there was a Centre near our town, so we got the London one from Directory Enquiries. (See *Useful Contacts*.) This is run by the Department of Industry. They answer any business problem, financial, technical or managerial. There are ten regional enquiry points so far. The service is entirely *free*, they put you in touch with a consultant whom you can phone and ask his fee before seeing him.'

### Ann

'I asked C.A.B. and they made an appointment for me to have a chat with an accountant free of charge. He told me I ought to employ an accountant to sort out the muddle I'd got into.'

## What does an accountant cost?

### Kate

'I decided to get an accountant in the end. He said his fee would be a minimum of £75 because all retail work is fiddly and slows him up. He thought in future his normal fee would be between £25 and £30 a quarter. I think it's worth it. It worries me if the book work gets into a mess.'

### Ann

'I pay my accountant now around £35 per quarter. I've found I need professional advice.'

## How to find an accountant

### Kate

'The Secretary, Institute of Chartered Accountants (see *Useful Contacts*) recommended someone to me.'

### Ann

On the advice of the C.A.B. Ann telephoned The Association of Certified & Corporate Accountants.

## Rates and insurance

### Kate

'My house is already insured; at least the ground floor which we occupy. At first I wanted to acquire the use of a room in the basement as a storeroom. But the accountant warned this would certainly increase our rates. So I'm going to manage in our own flat for the time being and see how it goes.'

### Ann

'My rates will be increased next year (over and above the expected increase) because of the "improvements" which the Council wanted: the new lavatory and washroom with a basin and hot and cold water. Also I've taken out an extra policy for the business.'

## How to get the money to invest

*Kate*
'I finally got a loan from the bank for £400 – with my husband's help.'

*Ann*
'The accountant told me to make an appointment to see my Bank Manager and to ask for a £2,000 loan.'

## Securities for loans?

*Kate*
Kate asked the Bank Manager what securities he would accept. 'He said they'd accept any shares we held, or a building society account, or any investment or a life insurance policy or a guarantee from my husband. Luckily we had a small sum in a building society joint account. They accepted this as security and we simply had to leave the pass book with the bank until the loan was paid off.'

*Ann*
'I offered the house, which is my own, as security and a Life Insurance Policy my parents bought for me some years ago; a very small one, but it all helped.'

## Bank interest on loans

*Kate*
'The Bank Manager suggested we settle the interest rate immediately, and we agreed a repayment term of 2 to 5 years. I get income tax relief on my loan because I could show I need the money strictly for business purposes.'

*Ann*
'I undertook to make a regular payment of so much a year until the loan is cleared. Payment was to start at about £70 to £100 per month, increasing annually by mutual agreement. This seems to be a fairly standard arrangement. My accountant told me I would get full income tax relief on the loan as the money was for the business. He also said I couldn't have got the tax relief if I'd wanted the money for a personal reason, other than for home improvements loans etc.'

## The bank

*Kate*
'I was advised to open a separate account for the business. This helps to keep an eye on bank charges.'

*Ann*
'I opened a separate account at my bank, a business current account. The trouble here was I always forgot to take both of my cheque books with me when I went shopping, so now I always keep them pinned together in a folder.'

105

# And Co. Ltd.

*Kate*

Kate thought of being a Company at first, naming her husband as director (which might have had certain tax advantages) but the accountant advised against it.

*Ann*

Ann's accountant also saw no advantage in her becoming a company unless her earnings passed the £7,000 a year mark. 'He said it would cost £20 a year to be a registered company and also there is a legal obligation to have the books audited. However, to be a limited company can be some protection for one's own home and possessions, so he said we could always review the situation later on.'

## Neighbours

*Kate*

'It was C.A.B. who advised me always to be discreet and tactful, and never to use my sewing machine at night as we live in a flat and have neighbours above.'

*Ann*

'Ann's nearest neighbour was half-a-mile away! The news about my cafe spread like wildfire in the surrounding area; this was good because I had a number of telephone calls from girls, including some schoolgirls asking to do part-time waitress work for me. It saved me a lot of money, not only in advertising for help, but because casual labour is so much cheaper.'

## Licensing

*Kate*

When Kate consulted C.A.B. she was told that a 'licence to work is usually necessary only where food or children are concerned'.

*Ann*

Ann telephoned the Environmental Officer at her Local Authority and her kitchen and outhouses have been approved so she is in the clear.

## Equipment

*Kate*

Kate made an inventory of her requirements and bought all her materials from a local upholsterer who is her first and largest customer. She is buying a big, workroom sewing-machine with attachments. (See *Upholstery* in Chapter 1.)

*Ann*

Ann bought a job lot of new china at reduced prices. Her problem was the large number of breakages and losses during the season, so she must replace a fair quantity each season. She tried buying plastic but this proved not popular. She also bought an assortment of chairs and tables.

106

## National Insurance contributions

*Kate*
'I asked C.A.B. how much I must pay for my insurance stamps weekly as a self-employed person, and they told me to call at my local Employment Office, where I was given Leaflet N1 41, March 1975 called *"National Insurance guidance for the self-employed"* which is clear and easy to understand.'

*Ann*
'In my first year my earnings were less than the then tax limit, so I was given for that year the Leaflet NL 27A which explains how my earnings were calculated for exemption purposes and advised how to apply for exemption. However, in the following year I had to employ a full-time waitress and felt uncertain what to do about her insurance contributions. C.A.B. advised me to contact my nearest Small Firms Information Centre which I did.' (See *Useful Contacts.*)

## Income Tax

*Kate*
'My accountant advised me to be taxed separately from my husband. He also gave me instructions on how to prepare my tax returns every April. Mind you, I still feel I could do with extra advice. It's a tricky subject.'

*Ann*
'Frankly, this was the hardest part for me. I hadn't a clue. I think it would be helpful to give a whole section on income tax advice because, although my accountant did tell me, I need to see it down in writing so that I can refer to it when necessary.'

I do so agree with both Kate and Ann on this point. So I'm cutting into Kate and Ann's story here with some simple rules which I'm calling 'Tax extra', to show it's all part of 'Organising'.

# Tax Extra

## How to cope with Income Tax and other problems

One mistake which both Kate and Ann happily avoided was keeping their earnings dark from the tax man. Don't make this mistake. To be found out could be humiliating and expensive. You could be fined a substantial sum.

So before examining what Kate and Ann did about it, please take note of a few general words of advice on this whole topic.

The chances are that if you 'come clean', H.M. Inspector of Taxes may let you keep all you've earned, unless you're making yourself a massive fortune! He does not – contrary to generally accepted opinion – want to put either you or your accountant out of business: this would only mean less revenue for him to collect. Just tell him all your troubles and even if you're the most fanatical womenslibber, don't be afraid of looking a bit helpless. The result will be that you can work with an easy mind and not have to worry about the little man next door who claims he's got some dull, unmentionable job in the City.

Did you know the favourite occupation of tax inspectors on rainy afternoons is browsing through the newspapers and magazines to see who is advertising what? You may be sure that some little man in the Tax Office will spot your innocent 'ad' in the local rag, offering some skilled sewing, gardening – or massage! Then there are all those little cards in newsagents windows; they can give you away too.

The truth is that it is to your own advantage to contact the tax man yourself. It will put the Inspector of Taxes on your side from the start. It shows you have nothing to hide. Besides, he just loves writing you chatty letters!

Of course, the inspector may be a woman and I mention this only because you might one day have a sudden urge to unbosom yourself to the woman living in the flat next door . . .

I've already said elsewhere in this chapter that you are allowed by law to earn £1,375 per annum entirely free of income tax, if that is your total income. But if you have any pension, alimony, dividends from investments, bank interest or any other income not listed, you must reveal it.

My own advice is to tell the tax inspector so much about your affairs that you very nearly bore him to death! Instead of trying to conceal this or that little item, do just the opposite. Tell him everything – how Granny gave you a fiver for Christmas and how expensive it was sending cards to customers. As long as you're telling the truth, it can do you nothing but good. Don't be afraid of opening your heart to the Inland Revenue; it may wear them out, poor chaps, or give them all a nervous breakdown but none of them will be able to say that *you* failed to give them what we call in the newspaper business 'a lovely long read'.

There is an extremely long list of 'allowable expenses' for the self-employed and it is entirely your own fault if you neglect to claim them. That is why you must keep all your receipts, however small or insignificant, safely in a file to send to the tax man . . . whether he asks to see them or not. Keep everything; even that used platform ticket you bought to see a customer safely on his way. Your accountant may reel at the thought of your forthcoming tax returns, and he may even charge you an extra £20 per hour's extra work for the sheer nuisance of checking your miserable bits and pieces (like the receipt for a box of 10p steel paper clips). Never mind, you will prove you're an honest woman and, what is more, you will get all the tax relief to which you are justly entitled.

Your first year of business will obviously be the most expensive because you are starting and because you are buying equipment, furnishing one room as your office; this may mean chairs, desk, reading-lamp, files and filing-cabinet perhaps. Proportions of your bills for heat, light and decorating are all allowable, and if your business means meeting a lot of new people you can charge a proportion for clothes and cosmetics – provided you can show that your handsome appearance is a necessity for your business. And of course it is! You've got to charm the tax man for a start.

*Useful Note:*
You can obtain useful advice on finance, loans, and so on from Female Financial Advisers Limited, Sedgwick House, 33 Aldgate High Street, London, EC3 N1AJ (Tel: 01-377 3456).

Now let's look at what Kate and Ann did

---

## First find your (tax) man

*Kate*
'I wrote to my husband's tax inspector, outlined my work plans and asked to be taxed separately.'

*Ann*
'I got Butterworth's Tax Handbook (10th Edition) from our local library. I wanted to know something about tax law, but I didn't understand much of it, so I asked C.A.B. for the phone number of the local Tax Office. I rang to get the address of the correct Tax Department for the area where I live. I was told to give my address, and later I received a letter from the office concerned, though it was in another part of the country.'

---

## Married or single?

*Kate*
'My accountant explained that it is not always beneficial to be taxed separately from a husband, but in my case he thought it would be. So I am taxed as a single, self-employed person under Schedule D.'

*Ann*
'I had nearly two years' back tax to pay. It was a relief to let my accountant sort it out. But I learned a lesson from this – never to get behind again with my accounts. I'm taxed as single, self-employed under Schedule D.'

## Filling in the tax form

*Kate*

'I find it easiest to pick on a date to prepare my accounts, and stick to that. So I know that on April 30th I've got to sit down and put my books in order. Unfortunately I can't type so I print it instead. As long as I keep my books in order throughout the year, I can get the job done in a week or ten days.

*Ann*

'I'm not a very orderly person. I try to start the first week in April and it takes me at least a month or longer to complete the books and expenses and petty cash accounts. The accountant explained that my tax assessments are based on my profits for each year. After two or three years have gone by, my tax for each year is based on my profit for the previous year; that is to say on my income after deducting expenses and allowances.'

'It's up to H.M. Inspector to argue what figures apply to which year.'

## Claims against tax

*Kate*

'I'm allowed to claim a proportion for depreciation of the large sewing-machine I bought secondhand and the small machine as well. I also claim for depreciation of all the smaller items like my sets of needles and shears and so on. As I use my car for the business, collecting and delivering materials, I claim for depreciation on that too. I claim for intermittent domestic help and for a babysitter when I have to complete orders in a rush. I claim a proportion for travel, and a proportion for light, heat and cleaning of my workroom, telephone, insurance and for my share of the mortgage payments as we're buying the flat.

'One year I lectured several times to a class of students and I claimed a proportion of my travel expenses and for a new dress, hat and coat.'

*Ann*

'I claim for depreciation of all my equipment – the new freezer, refrigerator, double oven, electric blender and my cake-mixer. I claim for my own clothes because I am receiving guests either as waitress or hostess, and for a proportion of my hair-do and manicure. I claim not only for depreciation, but also for damage (which is considerable). One season I had to replace all the cups and saucers and lots of the ashtrays which get taken away as souvenirs! I claim for depreciation of the carpets in the hall and indoor café. I also claim for my accountant's fees and for necessary shopping trips on business.'

# What to do with the tax form

(This arrives shortly before the start of the income-tax-year on April 5th.)

*Kate*
Kate sends hers straight on to her accountant. 'I supply the information he asks for, then he fills up the form, returns it to me for signature and then I send it back to him for sending to the tax man, together with a typed document of my profit and loss account, which he provides for me, all typed out in proper legal form.'

*Ann*
Ann also sends hers to her accountant. 'My business affairs are fairly complicated, so the accountant comes to see me. I find it easier to let him go through my books and accounts and do pretty well the whole thing himself. It means he charges me more, but I don't have the time (or the knowledge) to do it. I set his fees against tax.'

# Bank overdraft

*Kate*
'My business overdraft is allowable for tax purposes; (the accountant said it is only a "personal" overdraft which you can't claim for).'

*Ann*
'I had to have a business overdraft and I claim this against tax. Every little helps!'

# Bank interest on loans

*Kate*
'Interest on my business loan from the bank is also allowable for tax purposes, since I needed the money to buy my new sewing-machine and other equipment.'

*Ann*
'I'm allowed to charge against tax for the interest on the bank loan for the house improvements and all my new equipment.'

# Capital Gains Tax

This applies to both Kate and Ann. You must realise that if you own your own home and you use one room exclusively for business, you lose your exemption from C.G.T. whenever you sell your home.

## Valued Added Tax

Ann's earnings in teas and refreshments came perilously close to the V.A.T. level of £13,500 in her third season. By the time her accountant had set against that sum an amount of almost £5,000 in overhead expenses and wages for casual help, her takings were reduced to well below the level where V.A.T. has to be paid. However, when her bank loan is paid off, and if the business goes on increasing, Ann will have to learn about V.A.T. herself. So here's what it's all about.

*How to learn about V.A.T.*
Ann's accountant said she could read about it in two booklets provided by V.A.T. offices throughout Britain. (He also warned it's pretty difficult to understand.) He told her to get Booklet No. 700 which is the V.A.T. General Guide, and Booklet No. 701 on Scope and Coverage of V.A.T.

*How to get hold of V.A.T. booklets*
Ann looked up the address and phone number of H.M. Customs & Excise Office in her local telephone book. (C for Customs.) She telephoned and asked for the address of one of the many V.A.T. offices, so that she could call at or write to the nearest one to collect the booklets.

*How to assess whether you need to pay V.A.T.*
Don't bother if you're earning less than £15,000 per annum. But if your gross income is £15,000 or more, you must register with a V.A.T. office. Each quarter you have to work out whether you have earned over the limit which makes you liable for V.A.T. You must assess each quarter on January 1st, April 1st, July 1st, October 1st.

Look back over the previous quarters to assess whether you come under the quarter limit figures. *Note* These were revised on March 11th 1981. Now, if your income exceeds £5,000 in any one quarter, or if your annual turnover exceeds £15,000, then you are liable to pay V.A.T.

Before ending this section on tax problems, here are some notes concerning old-age pensioners.

## For old-age pensioners

Reduction in Income Tax (1980 figures): if a married couple has an income of £5,900 per annum or less, they are entitled to an allowance of £2,895 a year tax-free. There is an extra allowance for you, particularly if you have no other income, so make sure you get it. Even if your income exceeds this sum, you may still be entitled to a part of this – as opposed to the ordinary allowance of £2,145.

For a single person of 65 with an income of under £5,900 the allowance is £1,820.

If your income is over £5,900, the allowance is reduced by £2 for every £3 of income over £5,900.

# The Law

Some points covered in this chapter have already been dealt with under 'Organising'. Never mind, it won't hurt to remind you of your legal obligations.

Kate Barr consulted C.A.B. at the outset. Legal requirements for working at home vary according to the nature of the work. This list was put in front of her:

(a) Where the home-worker is a tenant (whether of a local authority or private landlord) or has a mortgage, she should examine the terms of her tenancy or mortgage.

(b) She should discuss with a reputable insurance firm whether she needs to take out special insurance cover for the business part of her premises and/or equipment.

(c) If the work requires structural changes to house or flat, plans must be approved by the local Planning Officer's Department, who will also want to check the work complies with building regulations.

(d) When handling food or livestock, the Public Health Department need to inspect the premises and to be satisfied as to hygiene regulations.

(e) Structural alterations to a property may lead to an increase in the rateable value of the property and hence a rise in rates.

At Kate's request, C.A.B. also arranged for her a free interview with a solicitor. He told her that as an outworker or freelance, she was entitled to the full protection of the law.

## Protection for outworkers at home

Kate's work was similar to that of an outworker because one particular upholsterer was employing her at home.

The lawyer told her that legislation in recent years has made firms and organisations employing outworkers just as responsible for your safety at work as if you were doing the job on their own factory premises.

The 1961 Factory Act requires employers in certain industries to submit twice-yearly lists of homeworkers to their local authority. The Health and Safety at Work Act has extended the registration requirements to cover all industrial outworkers. The local authority lists are available for inspection by authorised people such as Inspectors of the Health and Safety Executive and Wages Inspectors.

Not all firms, however, comply with these regulations. Some do not reveal the names of their outworkers. C.A.B's advice was 'if in doubt, please consult us about it.'

The lawyer advised Kate to consult C.A.B. before undertaking to buy any equipment, like a sewing-machine, knitting-machine or whatever, since there are some firms who promise work only because they want to persuade people to buy the machines. So always check with C.A.B. first.

Ann Aston's problems were different from Kate's. Ann was faced with structural alterations: the extra lavatory and washroom. Moreover her business had grown and developed in a short time to such an extent that the law concerning 'Change of Use' was soon involved. So C.A.B. again provided free legal advice.

## What the law says on 'Change of Use'

A change of use is considered to be

development for the purposes of Planning Permission and any building or alterations to the property may require Planning Permission.

There is a 120-page paperback book available on Planning Law. The basic proposition is that every property has a planning use, generally either as a result of a Planning Permission or of a long-established use.

In general terms the use of a property cannot be changed without Planning Permission, but property can be used for an ancillary purpose provided that it is not a material change of use. It is the definition of the word 'material' that is so difficult because every case depends on its own facts; some cases could be decided either way. The only possible method of being certain is for somebody intending to do this to speak to their local Planning Department and, if necessary, make a Planning Application. In general terms, there is no general objection to a non-industrial use (i.e. non-manufacturing, non-mechanical, non-retail), but it is very much up to the individual Planning Authority how far it is prepared to go.

A change of use is considered development for the purposes of Planning Permission, and obviously any building or alterations to the property may require Planning Permission.

If the Local Authority find out that a property was being used in contravention of the Act, they can either take the person concerned to court, or have them restrained from continuing the use. The answer is – if in doubt, always enquire first.

So you see, unless you plan to turn your whole house or flat into a sort of industrial factory, there's not much for you to worry about. The reason I have given a chapter and verse of this legal situation is that it may save you the expense of going to a solicitor. Armed with this knowledge, you will be able to make your own decisions.

Should you then decide that what you are doing is perfectly legal, and you don't need the permission of anyone at all, that's fine. As long as you use your common sense. Don't start putting little notices in the front parlour window saying 'Home-grown radishes sold here' or some such nonsense! You're allowed to advertise your political beliefs during an election with placards like 'Vote Labour' or 'Vote Tory' but if it's your garden radishes you want to promote, then you've got to get the Council's blessing.

When it comes to selling cooked food, there's no question. You must ask for permission. But even this can be done nearly painlessly. So I've devoted the whole of the next section to it. Please read on.

*What to do about cooked food*
If you plan to sell home-baked cakes, confectionery, sweets or other food you've cooked in your own kitchen, you must invite the Health Inspector to call.

I have been told by many women who have undergone this experience that it is perfectly simple, quick and trouble-free. The inspector calls, by appointment, looks shyly into your kitchen sink – rather like those 'ad' men do in the TV advertisements – and says something like 'yes, yes, how nice'. And that's it.

If you've announced your intention to cook for a living, and no one then turns up to see what's cooking, that's just too bad. You're in the clear.

Thousands of lucky British women can go ahead and cook the stuff and sell it without any of this fuss at all. These are the fortunate people who live either in rural areas or not too far from a country town which has a W.I. Market.

*How to avoid all the legal restrictions*
Over many years, the National Federation of Women's Institutes have gone to a lot of trouble to negotiate with the authorities concerned. They have done

their legal homework and made their own rules about how a woman should use her own kitchen to sell her own produce.

By becoming a member (which won't cost you much) you too can avoid all the legal fuss of asking permission from your Local Authority. But you must sell your produce in one of the W.I. Markets. You will recall the recent fuss in Parliament when some idiot claimed that even W.I. *jam* was illegal. That got sorted out eventually. But be clever! Avoid clashing with the 'Law'. Tell the food inspector to 'come and have Dinner any time,' just to show you're not scared of him!

Local Authorities' main concern is to avoid salmonella or any other kind of food poisoning. There's a lot of it about. That's why the law is so strict on selling cooked food.

The W.I. Market is an excellent outlet so, if you have no Market near your home, then start a group with friends of yours and open your own Market. Write to the National Federation of Women's Institutes, 39 Eccleston Street, London, SW1W 9NT, and they will tell you how to do it.

There are 300 W.I. Markets in the United Kingdom, and most of them are near enough to cities to be accessible. New W.I. Markets are being opened all the time.

### Food and what to do about it

If, therefore, you are planning to do one of the jobs listed earlier which has anything to do with food – then proceed as follows:

1. First write a letter to your local Environmental Health Officer at the Council Offices. Tell him that as your home-made scones are so popular with friends and neighbours, you propose to widen your scope a bit and sell them in the area to people who want to buy them.

2. Tell him that you are writing to let him know your plans in accordance with the Food Hygiene Act, the Weights and Measures Act, the Trades Description Act and all statutory regulations for the sale and presentation of all types of produce. (That should show him he is dealing with a woman who knows what she's at.)

3. Tell him that he is welcome to come and see your kitchen at any time he likes, if he'll kindly ring or write to make an appointment first so he doesn't have a wasted journey. (You can even make him a cup of tea and throw in one of your home-baked scones for good measure.)

Now you are in the clear, you can go ahead. He may come or he may not. If he doesn't turn up for the next five years, that's not your fault. You've obeyed the rules, and that's what matters.

4. Tell him that you propose to start this work meanwhile, in strict accordance with the statutory regulations adhered to by the National Federation of Women's Institutes as given in their current booklet called *The W.I. Market Handbook*. (Ask for this at your library or write to your nearest W.I. office for a copy.)

### Some of the statutory regulations

Produce must be absolutely fresh and of good quality. When selling by weight, measure or number, goods that are not prepacked, the scales must be visible to the customer. Scales must be accurate. Measuring and counting must be done in the presence of the customer.

Other rules cover: Food Hygiene, Definition of Prepack, Protection of Food, Personal Cleanliness, Deep Freezing and so on . . .

### Trades Description Act

Under the Act, goods offered for sale must be labelled accurately, i.e. if the label states 'Butter Icing', this must have been made with butter and not margarine.

### The Health Inspector

If and when he comes, watch these points:

Don't have cats, dogs or other pets in the kitchen.

Keep foods separate from each other.

Don't use newspapers for wrapping.

Show that you have adequate washing facilities.

Have a nice clean look all over: clean hands and clean pinny, clean fingernails, no hanging hair. If you stick to all this good advice from the W.I. you'll always be, believe me, strictly legitimate, my daughter!

*Footnote:*
It is (so far) just a dream of mine that Parliament will decide now the State can no longer afford hot dinners for schoolchildren, that decent, clean British housewives who live near schools, should cook for them and make a modest profit by doing this 'at home'. Why not?

# Part Three

# The art of communication

There are still many people who do not know how to use the telephone.

'Citizen's Advice Bureau speaking.'

'Is that the Citizen's Advice Bureau?'

'Yes, C.A.B. here. Can I help you?'

'You can.'

'What is your query please.'

'It isn't a query; it's trouble with the next door dog.'

'Shall we start with your name please?'

'Oh no, I don't want to give my name. I don't know you.'

'Very well then. How can we help you?'

'I keep telling you. They keep letting the dog out . . .'

'Yes, go on, I'm listening.'

'That is someone from the Citizen's Advice speaking?'

'Yes . . . would you like to come and see us?'

'If you don't hurry up, my two-pence'll be all gone . . .'

I'm not suggesting that you would ever conduct a telephone conversation like that. But there are still a lot of people who don't know how to use a telephone. Some of the worst offenders are the very people who call themselves by the title telephonists:

YOU: 'Is that R. H. Smith Ltd?'

TELEPHONIST: 'No, it's not.'

YOU: 'You are not R. H. Smith Ltd?'

TELEPHONIST: 'I said it once, didn't I.'

YOU: 'I was given your number for R. H. Smith Ltd.'

TELEPHONIST: 'What number?'

YOU: '444 8877.'

TELEPHONIST: 'This is 444 8877'

YOU: 'Then you must be R. H. Smith Ltd.'

TELEPHONIST: 'No, we're not; you must want somebody else.'

YOU: 'Then who are you please?'

TELEPHONIST: 'We're not R. H. Smith Ltd. We're R. F. Smith Ltd.'

YOU: 'That's it! Put me through please to Mr. Smith.'

TELEPHONIST: 'I can't put you through, can I? We haven't got a Mr. R. H.'

YOU: 'Then I'll try Mr. R. F.'

TELEPHONIST: 'Have it your own way. It's your money you're wasting . . . hold the line.'

**Telephoning for advice:** If you are phoning a doctor, lawyer, Council officer, bank manager, businessman or woman or almost anyone, it is a good idea to ascertain first that you have not chosen a bad moment to put your case. Remember you are the one who is trespassing on their time. You want the benefit of their advice; be gracious and ask whether it is a convenient time to put your question. 'Am I disturbing you?' is the best possible start. Get yourself a good telephone reputation, otherwise people will try to avoid any future calls from you.

Try and imitate Ann Astons' near-perfect telephone manner.

ANN: 'Citizens Advice Bureau? Can you help me?'

C.A.B.: 'Yes?'

ANN: 'I have a man from the Council calling . . .'

C.A.B.: 'Yes?'

ANN: 'Can you prepare me for questions and so on?'

119

C.A.B.: 'What are the circumstances?'
ANN: 'My private premises are changed to a business.'
C.A.B. 'If you like to call?'
ANN: 'The visit is today.'
C.A.B.: 'Give me your phone number; I'll ring you back in five minutes with all the details you need to know.'
ANN: 'That is very kind.'

Always give your name, state your business briefly; always ask the name of the person who is speaking. Ask also for the correct name of their department and their extension number so that you can get through swiftly to them in future.

Gush a little when telephoning officialdom: 'I would be so glad of your advice,' or 'I hate to disturb you . . . but I badly need your help,' or 'My name is Smith. Excuse my taking up your time but I have a problem which I can state quite briefly.'

While telephone charges remain sky-high, you have to aim at uttering only the important words. That is, be brief and curt but use your silkiest manner. Make the voice a little ingratiating. In British business, this is liked. Even the customer is expected to be a little humble in Britain.

In the second year, when business is starting to swing, you can afford to relax a little. Discuss the weather or the customer's lumbago. Not yours. Never yours.

When telephoning any Civil Service Department, say firmly right at the start 'Please do not leave me waiting on the line. I am paying for this call.'

Avoid being trapped by the girl or man who answers the phone and wants to know all your business before putting you through to the boss. Your business is with the boss; so don't waste money telling the story twice. Instead say something like: 'It's a personal problem. I mustn't bore you or take up your busy time.'

It is a good idea to adopt your own personalised telephone style so that your voice is instantly recognisable. 'Kate Barr' she always says on lifting the receiver. It works like a signal of what's coming; a system the radio programmes always use.

Keep phone calls and letters short. If your letter to the Bank Manager or Council man runs to more than three paragraphs, there is something wrong with it. Rewrite and cut!

**Letters**

Kate Barr wrote to her bank manager after first ringing the bank to get his full name and initials and the correct spelling.

Dear Mr. Smith,

I work at home as an upholsterer and have a separate business account with you, number (     ). I now find I need a loan to purchase necessary equipment and shall telephone your secretary for an appointment early in the coming week.

Yours sincerely,

(Mrs.) Kate Barr


Ann got the name of the Environmental Health Officer at her local Council by telephoning C.A.B., who gave her his full name, title, department and address.

Dear Mr. Jones,

I am advised to contact you about the teas/refreshments garden café I opened recently at my home, the White Forge, which is a mile from the main A24 road near the junction with Reigate Road.

I need your advice on how to proceed within the local bye-laws and in accordance with regulations and shall therefore welcome a visit from you at your earliest convenience. I shall be obliged if you will kindly telephone in advance to make an appointment.

Yours sincerely,

(Miss) Ann Aston

# Useful Contacts

Please remember: a lot of these are voluntary organisations, run on a shoestring; send a stamped self-addressed envelope.

**Antiques Market,** Basement, 141 Notting Hill Gate. Mon-Fri, 10 a.m.–6 p.m. Stall enquiries Tel: 01-229 6360.

**Art Information Registry,** 125/129 Shaftesbury Avenue, London WC2H 8AD (Tel: 01-240 3149)

**Association of Certified Accountants,** 22 Bedford Square, London WC1B 3HS (Tel: 01-636 2103)

**Association of Home Economists Limited,** 192–8 Vauxhall Bridge Road, London SW1X 1DX (Tel: 01-821 6421)

**Association of Master Upholsterers,** Dormar House, Mitre Bridge, Scrubs Lane, London NW10 (Tel: 01-965 3565)

**Back Pain Association,** Grundy House, 31–33 Park Road, Teddington, Middx TW11 0AB. (London now has 30 Back Pain groups.)

**Beauty Without Cruelty International,** 1 Calverley Park, Tunbridge Wells (Tel: Tunbridge Wells 25587)

**BBC,** Broadcasting House, Portland Place, London W1A 1AA

**BBC Publications Dept,** 35 Marylebone High Street, London W1M 4AA

**BBC Radio Drama Dept,** Broadcasting House (as above)

**Books and Bookmen,** 75 Victoria Street, London SW1 (Tel: 01-799 4452)

**Brass Tacks Workshop,** 18 Ashwin Street, London E8 (Tel: 01-249 9461) (Workshops all over UK for recycling unwanted furniture and electrical appliances. For information write to: Mutual Aid Centre, 18 Victoria Park Square, London E2 9PF).

**British Antiques Dealers' Association,** 20 Rutland Gate, London SW7 1BD (Tel: 01-589 4128/2102)

**British Association of Accountants and Auditors,** Stamford House, 2 Chiswick High Road, London W4 1TP (Tel: 01-994 3477)

**British Copyright Protection Association,** 29 Berners Street, London W1 (Tel: 01-636 1491)

**British Federation of Business and Professional Women,** 3 Milk Street, London EC2 (Tel: 01-606 1961)

**British Goat Society,** Rougham, Bury St Edmunds, Suffolk

**British Nursing Association,** Freepost, London W1E 3Y2.

**British Property Federation,** 35 Catherine Place, London SW1E 6DY (Tel: 01-828 0111)

**British Tourist Association** (Tel: 01-629 9191 (admin)).

**British Toy Manufacturing Association,** 80 Camberwell Road, London SE5

**Cats:** Expert on breeding. Mrs. Alison Ashford, Annelida, Roundwell, Bearsted, Maidstone, Kent (Tel: 0622 37050)

**Central Bureau for Educational Visits and Exchanges,** 43 Dorset Street, London W1H 3FN (Tel: 01-486 5101)

**Charity Christmas Card Council,** 84 Southampton Row, London WC1 (Tel: 01-242 0546)

**Chiropody Schools:** *Birmingham;* Matthew Boulton Technical College, Sherlock Street, Birmingham B5 7DH (Tel: 021-440 2681) Head: D. A.Haywood. *Chelsea* School of Chiropody, 18 Stamford Street, London NW8 8EN (Tel: 01-402 5621),

Head: P. H. Read. *Durham* School of Chiropody, Framwell Gate Moor, Durham DH1 5ES (Tel: 0385 62421), Head: A. Robertson. *Huddersfield* The Polytechnic, Queensgate, Huddersfield HD1 3DH (Tel: 0484 22288), Head: M. F. Whiting. *London* Foot Hospital, School of Chiropody, 33 Fitzroy Square, London W1P 6AY (Tel: 01-636 0602), Principal: L. A. Smidt. *Manchester* Northern College of Chiropody, Salford College of Technology, Frederick Road, Salford M6 6PU (Tel: 061-736 6541). Manchester Annexe, 5–7 Anson Road, Victoria Park, Manchester M14 5BR (Tel: 061-224 2229), Head of College: T. P. Bradley. *Plymouth* School of Chiropody, College of Further Education, North Road West, Plymouth, PL1 5BY (Tel: 0752 21312), Head of School: D. J. Ashcroft. *Northern Ireland* Northern Ireland School of Chiropody, College of Technology, College Square East, Belfast BT1 6DJ. *Scotland* Edinburgh Foot Clinic and School of Chiropody, 81 Newington Road, Edinburgh EH9 1QW (Tel: 031-667 3197/9241), Principal: Miss M. H. Price. Glasgow School of Chiropody 757 Crookston Road, Glasgow G53 7UA (Tel: 041-883 0418/0419), Principal: C. Feebairn. *Wales* Cardiff School of Chiropody, South Glamorgan Institute of Higher Education, Cardiff CF5 2YB (Tel: 0222 561241), Head: D. F. Jesset.

**Church of England Children's Society,** Old Town Hall, Kennington Road, London SE11 4QD (Tel: 01-735 2441). Regional Offices include: (*North*) Social Work Office, 37 Fishergate, York YO1 4AP (Tel: 0904 27866); (*North-West*) Social Work Office, The Bungalow, Rear of Ingledene, Richmond Road, Bowden, Cheshire (Tel: 061-928 9120); (*Midlands*) S.W. Office, 111 Church Hill Road, Handsworth, Birmingham (Tel: 021-523 9029); (*Eastern*) S.W. Office, 21 Dunstable Road, Luton, Beds. (Tel: 0582 33832); (*Wales*) S.W. Office, Wick House, Wick Road, Brislington, Bristol (Tel: 0272 773781).

**Christine Shaw Company,** 11 Old Bond Street, London W1X 3DB (Tel: 01-629 3884/5)

**Citizens' Advice Bureaux:** there are 675 in the United Kingdom, listed in local telephone directories. Addresses and hours of opening obtainable from town halls, post office and public libraries. (Some places are covered by mobile C.A.B. units.)

*Headquarters:* The National Association of Citizens' Advice Bureaux, 110 Drury Lane, London, W2B 5SW (Tel: 01-636 4066)

**College of Horticulture,** New Common Bridge, Wisbech, Cambridgeshire PR13 2SJ (Tel:Wisbech 2561, ex 246/7)

**Commercial Rabbit Association,** Tyning House, Shurdington, Cheltenham, Glos. (Tel: Cheltenham 387)

**Cordon Bleu Cookery School,** 114 Marylebone Lane, London W1 (Tel: 01-935 3503)

**Constance Spry School,** 74 Marylebone Lane, London W1 (Tel: 01-499 7201)

**'Contact',** The UK News Contact Directory, Windsor Court, East Grinstead House, East Grinstead, West Sussex RH19 1XA (Tel: 0342 26972)

**Council for Dance Education and Training,** 5 Tavistock Place, London WC1 (Tel: 01-388 5770)

**Council for the Accreditation of Correspondence Colleges,** 27 Marylebone Road, London NW1 5JS (They will supply a list of accredited colleges which includes a brief description of each college's subjects.) (Tel: 01-935 5391)

**COSIRA** (The government-sponsored Council for Small Industries in Rural Areas), 141 Cowley Street, Salisbury, Wilts, SP1 3TP. COSIRA in Wales: Welsh Development Agency, Treforest, Pontypridd, Mid Glamorgan, South Wales (Tel: 0443 852666); Development Business Agency, Ladywell House, Newtown, Powys SY16 1JB (Tel: 0686 26965). COSIRA in Scotland: Scottish Small-Business

Agency, 102 Telford Road, Edinburgh EH4 2NP (Tel: 031-343 1911/1916).

**Crafts,** *For courses of training;* West Dean College, West Dean, Chichester, West Sussex; Styal Workshop, Quarry Bank Mill, Styal, Cheshire, SK9 4LA (send s.a.e. for prospectus); Earnley Concourse, Near Chichester, Sussex PO20 7JL (send s.a.e. for brochure); The Field Studies Council, Preston Montford, Montford Bridge, Shrewsbury; Booking Secretary, Dillington House College, (For Adult Education and Arts Centre) Ilminster, Somerset, TA19 9DT; The National Institute of Adult Education, 19b De Montfort Street, Leicester, LE1 7GE (send 60p for a booklet about their residential short courses).

**Debt Counselling:** booklet available from the Birmingham Settlement Money Advice Centre, 318 Summer Lane, Birmingham B19 3RL

**Denman College,** Marcham, Abingdon, Oxfordshire OX13 6NW (Tel: Frillford Heath 219 and 425)

**Design Council,** 28 Haymarket, London SW1 (Tel: 01-839 8000)

**Dolls:** Mrs. Daphne Fraser, 'Glenbarry', 58 Victoria Road, Lenzie, Near Glasgow (Tel: 041-776 1281)

**Department of Employment,** (headquarters) Caxton House, Tothill Street, London SW1 (Tel: 01-213 3000)

**En Famille Agency,** Westbury House, Queens Lane, Arundel, Sussex (Tel: Arundel 882450)

**English Tourist Board,** (Special Interests, Recreation) Booklet price 70p from The English Tourist Board, 4 Grosvenor Gardens, London SW1W 0DU.

**Federation of Personnel Services of Great Britain Limited,** 120 Baker Street, London W1M 2DE (Tel: 01-487 5250)

**Feline Advisory Bureau,** Cats' Hotel, Orcheston, Nr Salisbury, Wilts. (Send a £2.18 postal order with your letter.)

**Female Financial Advisers,** Sedgewick House, 33 Aldgate High Street, London EC3N 1AJ (Tel: 01-377 3456)

**Fred Aldous Limited,** The Handicraft Centre, P.O. Box 135, 37 Lever Street, Manchester M60 1UX (Tel: 061-236 2477)

**Gabbitas-Thring Educational Trust,** Broughton House 6/7/8 Sackville Street, London W1 (Tel: 01-734 0165)

**Guild of Guides and Lecturers,** General Secretary, Mrs Helen Clapp, Blackfriars Lane, London EC4V 6ER (Tel: 01-248 7752)

**Guild of Weavers, Spinners and Dyers,** Mrs. C. M. Laycock (secretary), Five Bays, 10 Stancliffe Avenue, Marford, Wrexham, Clwyd.

**Hairdressing Council,** 17 Spring Street, London W2 (Tel: 01-402 6367)

**Hairdressing Schools:** Alan Hairdressing International, 54 Knightsbridge, London SW1; Vidal School of Hairdressing, 56 Davies Mews, London W1; Morris Mast Class, 247 Tottenham Court Road, London W1; Midland Academy of Hair Fashion, 24 Albert Street, Birmingham; Southern School of Hairdressing, 136 London Road, Brighton, Sussex; The Private College of Careers, 109 Queen Street, Cardiff; Brian Drum Hair Academy, 57 George Street, Edinburgh 2; House of Hair, 4 Hope Street, West End, Edinburgh; St George's School of Hairdressing, 73 St George's Road, Glasgow; Yorkshire College of Hairdressing, 103 Kirkgate, Leeds 2; Excel Salons Hairdressing School, 5 Central Building, Market Place Appoach, Leicester; The Clark School of Hairdressing, 140 Deansgate, Manchester; The Elegant Hair Academy, Lancaster Buildings, Barton Square, Manchester; Romanoff College of Hairdressing, 34 Moorfields, Liverpool; Great Yarmouth College of Further Education, (Hairdressing Appointments), Great Yarmouth; Vogue School of Hairdressing, 2 Glamis Street, Bognor Regis, West Sussex; Sheffield Institute of Hairdressing, 160 Devonshire Street, Sheffield 3; Aquarius Academy, 57 St Helen's Road, Swansea, West Glamorgan.

**Health & Social Security, Department of,** (general enquiries), Alexander Fleming House, Elephant and Castle, London SE1 (Tel: 01-407 5522)

**Homebound Craftsmen Trust,** 29 Holland Street, Kensington, London W8 (Tel: 01-937 3924)

**H.M.S.O.** (Stationery Office), P.O. Box 569, London SE1 (Tel: 01-928 1321)

**Institute of Chartered Accountants** (England and Wales), P.O. Box 433, Moorgate Place, London EC2P 2BJ (Tel: 01-628 7060) (Scotland) 66 Cannon Street, London EC4

**International Correspondence School,** Intertext House, 160 Stewarts Road, London SW8 4UJ (Tel: 01-622 9911)

**Institute of Incorporated Photographers,** Amwell End, Ware, Herts. SG12 9HN (Tel: Ware 4011)

**Institute of Linguists,** 24a Highbury Grove, London N5 2EA (Tel: 01-359 7445)

**International Computers Limited** (Contract Programming Services), Westfields, West Avenue, Kidsgrove, Stoke-on-Trent STU 1TL (Tel: Stoke-on-Trent 29681)

**Kennel Club,** 1–4 Clarges Street, London W1 (Tel: 01-493 6651)

**KIEWE,** Heinz Edgar (for advice on books on knitting) from A.N.I. Limited, Ship Street, Oxford

**Kleeneze Limited,** Ansteys Road, Hanham, Bristol, BS15 3DY (Tel: 0272 670861)

**Knitmaster Limited,** 30–40 Elcho Street, London SW1 (Tel: 01-228 9303)

**Laura Ashley,** 40 Sloane Street, London SW1 (for furnishing fabrics); 71 Lower Sloane Street, London SW1 (for dress fabrics). There are also branches round the country.

**Libraries:** to save yourself useless journeys, it is often worthwhile making a phone call to your local central reference library to check whether the book or magazine you require is available. The librarian will have a list of phone numbers of other libraries; and may well be able to tell you where you will find what you want.

**Library Association,** 7 Ridgmont Street, London WC1E 7AE (Tel: 01-637 7543)

**London College of Fashion and Design,** 20 John Prince's Street, London W1M 9HE (Tel: 01-493 8341)

**London Foot Hospital,** 33 Fitzroy Square, London W1 (Tel: 01-636 0602)

**Market Research Society,** 15 Belgrave Square, London SW1X 8PF (Tel: 01-235 4709)

**Marriage Guidance Council,** 76a New Cavendish Street, London W1 (Tel: 01-580 1087)

**Museums:** many museums offer lectures on various aspects of their collections, and they can be the source of ideas for design in practically every field. There are 27 listed under 'Museum' in the London phone book alone, covering everything from furniture to industrial health and safety! There is a Museum of Costume in Bath, and a Museum of Childhood in Edinburgh (it is opposite John Knox's house); in York you will find reconstructed streets, with period shop fronts; there is a Museum of Industrial Archaeology at Coalbrookdale. Museum of Childood, 38 High Street, Edinburgh (Tel: 031-556 5447), open Mon-Sat: 10 a.m.–5 p.m. Oct.-Mar., Jun.-Sept. 10 a.m.–6 p.m. Children 10p, Adults 30p (see also Daphne Fraser).

**National Advisory Centre on Careers for Women** Drayton Gardens, 30 Gordon Street, London WC1 (Tel: 01-380 0117)

**National Childbirth Trust,** 9 Queensborough Terrace, London W12 3TB (Tel: 01-221 3833)

**National Federation of Women's Institutes,** 39 Eccleston Street, London SW1W 9NT (Tel: 01-730 7212)

**National Foster-Care Association,** Francis House, Francis Street, London SW1.

**National Trust** (membership department), P.O. Box 30, Beckenham, Kent BR3 4TL (Tel: 01-650 7263). Junior division, for Acorn Camps, under-21 group membership and under-23 individual membership, The Old Grape

House, Cliveden, Taplow, Maidenhead, Berks, SL6 0HZ (Tel: Burnham, Bucks, 4228). Head office at 42 Queen Anne's Gate, London SW1H 9AS (Tel: 01-930 1841/0211)

**National Union of Journalists** (Freelance Branch) Acorn House, 314 Gray's Inn Road, London WC1 (Tel: 01-278 1812)

**National Union of Townswomen's Guilds** (for advice on art and craftwork etc), 2 Cromwell Place, South Kensington, London SW7 2JG (Tel: 01-589 8817/8/9)

**Nursing and Hospital Careers Information Centre,** 121/123 Edgware Road, London W2 (Tel: 01-402 5296 7)

**Office of Population Censuses and Surveys,** Social Survey Division, St. Catherine's House, 10 Kingsway, London WC2B 6JP (Tel: 01-242 0262, *Patent Office*, Department of Trade, 25 Southampton Buildings, London (Tel: 01-405 8721)

**Pippa-Dee Parties Limited,** Anglesey House, Anglesey Road, Burton-on-Trent DE14 3QD (Tel: Burton-on-Trent 66344)

**Quilters' Guild** (information from Margaret Petit), 32 Oxford Road, Farnborough, Hants.

**Pre-School Playgroups Association,** Alford House, Aveline Street, London SE11 5DH (Tel: 01-582 8871)

**Register of Approved Driving Instructors,** Department of Transport, 2 Marsham Street, London SW1 (Tel: 01-212 3434)

**Registrar of Business Names,** Pembroke House, 40/56 City Road, London EC1 (Tel: 01-253 9393)

**Royal Academy of Music,** Marylebone Road, London NW1 (Tel: 01-935 5461)

**Royal College of Music,** Prince Consort Road, London SW7 (Tel: 01-589 3643)

**Royal College of Nursing,** Henrietta Place, Cavendish Square, London W1M 0AB (Tel: 01-580 2646)

**Rural Music Schools Association,** Little Benslow Hills, Hitchin, Herts SG4 9RB (Tel: Hitchin 59446)

**Sales Force Limited,** 1 Berners Street, London W1 (Tel: 01-637 1444)

**School of Dressmaking and Design,** 69 Wells Street, London W1 (Tel: 01-580 9018)

**Servicemaster Limited,** 50 Commercial Square, Freeman's Common, Leicester LE2 7SR

**Small Firms Information Centres** (there are ten regional enquiry points in: Birmingham, Bristol, Cardiff, Glasgow, Leeds, London, Luton, Manchester, Newcastle and Nottingham. Each centre has a 24-hour answering service.) London: 65 Buckingham Palace Road, London SW1W 0QX (Tel: 01-828 2384)

**Small Landlords Association,** Rosedean Avenue, London SW16

**Society of Authors,** 85 Drayton Gardens, London SW10 (Tel: 01-373 6642)

**Society of Beauticians,** 29 Old Bond Street, London W1

**Society of Chiropodists,** 8 Wimpole Street, London W1

**Society of Dyers and Colourists,** 19 Piccadilly, Bradford (Tel: Bradford 25138)

**Society of Genealogists,** 37 Harrington Gardens, London SW7 4JX (Tel: 01-373 7054)

**Society of Indexers,** 7a Parker Street, Cambridge, CB1 1JL

**Spirella Fashion Service in the Home,** Bridge Road, Letchworth, Herts SG6 4ET (Tel: Letchworth 6161)

**Tax:** for enquiries on Income Tax, look in telephone directory under 'Inland Revenue'

**Taxation and Accountancy Services,** Monument Station Buildings, 53/54 King William Street, London EC4R 9AA (Tel: 01-623 6150)

**Telephone Selling:**

**The Toy Libraries Association** (publishers of *The Good Toy Guide*), Seabrook House, Darkes Lane, Potters Bar, Herts.

**Transport, Department of** (headquarters) 2 Marsham Street, London SW1 (Tel: 01-212 3434)

**Travel Information:** railway stations

are under 'British Rail' in the phone book

*Stations*
Charing Cross: 01-928 5100
Euston: 01-387 7070
Kings Cross: 01-837 3355
Liverpool St: 01-283 7171
Paddington: 01-262 6767
Victoria: 01-928 5100
Waterloo: 01-928 5100

*Airports*
Heathrow: 01-759 4321
Gatwick: 0293 31299

*Coaches*
Victoria Coach Station: 01:7300 0202

**Trades Advisory Council,** 44 Gray's Inn Road, London WC1 (Tel: 01-405 3188)

**Translators' Association,** 84 Drayton Gardens, London SW10 (Tel: 01-373 6642)

**Tupperware Company Limited,** Tupperware House, 43 Upper Grosvenor Street, London W1V 0BE (Tel: 01-629 7861)

**U.K. Press Gazette,** Cliffords Inn (Lower Ground Floor), Fetter Lane, London EC4 (Tel: 01-242 0935)

**Wages Council,** 12 St James's Square, London SW1Y 4LL (Tel: 01-214 6537/ 6112)

**Writers' Guild of Great Britain,** 430 Edgware Road, London W2 (Tel: 01-723 8074)

**Women's Institute:** *see above*, under National Federation of, *and* Denman College.

# Index

*If you can't find what you want in the* Index, *try* Useful Contacts. *You will find full addresses and telephone numbers there for many organisations.*